The Little Book of
Stoicism

*Timeless Wisdom to Gain
Resilience, Confidence,
and Calmness*

Jonas Salzgeber

Contents

Introduction   1

PART 1: WHAT IS STOICISM   9

Chapter 1: The Promise of Stoic Philosophy   11

Practice the Art of Living: Become a Warrior-
Philosopher   12

Promise #1: Eudaimonia   14

Promise #2: Emotional Resilience   17

Tame Restricting Emotions (≠ Unemotional)   19

Practice Stoicism and Become more Tranquil as a
By-Product   23

Chapter 2: A Quick History Lesson   26

The Most Important Stoic Philosophers   29

Seneca the Younger (c. 4 BCE – 65 CE)   30

Musonius Rufus (c. 30 CE – c. 100 CE)   32

Epictetus (c. 55 CE – c. 135 CE)   33

Marcus Aurelius (121 CE – 180 CE)   34

Chapter 3: The Stoic Happiness Triangle   36

The Stoic Happiness Triangle in A Nutshell   38

**1. Live with Areté: Express Your Highest Self in Every
Moment**   40

The Perfection of Our Natural Potential   43

The Four Cardinal Virtues   47

Character Beats Beauty   51

The Stoic Love of Mankind: Act for the Common
Welfare   53

2. Focus on What You Control: Accept Whatever Happens and Make the Best Out of It   **56**

The Stoic Archer: Focus on the Process   60

Stoic Acceptance: Enjoy the Ride or Get Dragged Along   63

The Good, the Bad, and the Indifferent Things   67

In Poker as in Life, You Can Win with Any Hand   71

3. Take Responsibility: Get Good from Yourself   **73**

The Freedom of Choice   76

The Mind Makes You Rich, Even in Exile   80

Disturbed or Invincible: That's Up to You   83

Chapter 4: The Villain: Negative Emotions Get in the Way   **87**

We Want What's Beyond Our Control   92

We Lack Awareness and Get Carried Away by Impressions   94

PART 2: 55 STOIC PRACTICES   **99**

Chapter 5: How to Practice Stoicism?   **101**

Brace Yourself   103

Be Mindful   104

Recharge Your Self-Discipline   106

Don't Call Yourself a Philosopher   107

Chapter 6: Preparing Practices   **109**

Practice 1 The Stoic Art of Acquiescence: Accept and Love Whatever Happens   110

Practice 2 Undertake Actions with a Reserve Clause   114

Practice 3 What Stands in the Way Becomes the Way   117

Practice 4 Remind Yourself of the Impermanence of Things   120

Practice 5 Contemplate Your Own Death   123

Practice 6 Consider Everything as Borrowed from Nature   125

Practice 7 Negative Visualization: Foreseeing Bad Stuff   128

Practice 8 Voluntary Discomfort   131

Practice 9 Prepare Yourself for the Day: The Stoic Morning Routine   134

Practice 10 Review Your Day: The Stoic Evening Routine   137

Practice 11 Keep a Role Model in Mind: Contemplate the Stoic Sage   140

Practice 12 Stoic Aphorisms: Keep Your "Weapons" Ready at Hand   143

Practice 13 Play Your Given Roles Well   146

Practice 14 Eliminate the Nonessential   149

Practice 15 Forget Fame   151

Practice 16 Like a Minimalist: Live Simple   153

Practice 17 Take Back Your Time: Cut Out News and Other Timewasters   156

Practice 18 Win at What Matters   159

Practice 19 Become an Eternal Student   162

Practice 20 What Do You Have to Show for Your Years?   165

Practice 21 Do What Needs to Get Done   168

Chapter 7: Situational Practices: How to Deal with Yourself When Life Gets Tough?   **171**

Practice 22 Your Judgment Harms You   173

Practice 23 How to Deal With Grief   175

Practice 24 Choose Courage and Calm over Anger   178

Practice 25 Beat Fear with Preparation and Reason   182

Practice 26 Blame Your Expectations   185

Practice 27 Pain and Provocation: Great Opportunities
for Virtue   188

Practice 28 The Equanimity Game   191

Practice 29 The Anti-Puppet Mindset   194

Practice 30 Life Is Supposed to Be Challenging   197

Practice 31 What's so Troublesome *Here and Now*?   200

Practice 32 Count Your Blessings   203

Practice 33 Other-ize   205

Practice 34 Take the Bird's-Eye View   208

Practice 35 It's the Same Old Things   210

Practice 36 Meat Is Dead Animal: Observe Objectively

212

Practice 37 Avoid Rashness: Test Your Impressions   215

Practice 38 Do Good, Be Good   219

**Chapter 8: Situational Practices: How to Handle Yourself
When Other People Challenge You?   222**

Practice 39 We Are All Limbs of the Same Body   224

Practice 40 Nobody Errs on Purpose   226

Practice 41 Find Your Own Faults   229

Practice 42 Forgive and Love Those Who Stumble   231

Practice 43 Pity Rather than Blame the Wrongdoer   234

Practice 44 Kindness Is Strength   237

Practice 45 How to Deal with Insults   239

Practice 46 Scratches Happen In Training   243

Practice 47 Don't Abandon Others nor Yourself   246

Practice 48 For Such a Small Price, Buy Tranquility 249

Practice 49 Put Yourself in Other People's Shoes   251

Practice 50 Choose Your Company Well   254

Practice 51 Don't Judge But Yourself   257
Practice 52 Do Good, Not Only No Evil   260
Practice 53 Say Only What's Not Better Left Unsaid   263
Practice 54 Listen with the Intent to Understand   265
Practice 55 Lead by Example   267

Acknowledgments   *271*
Selected Bibliography   *272*
Want More?   *275*

The Power of Philosophy

"The power of philosophy to blunt the blows of fate is beyond belief. No missile can settle in her body; she is well-protected and impenetrable. She spoils the force of some missiles and wards them off with the loose folds of her dress, as if they had no power to harm; others she dashes aside, and throws them back with such force that they rebound upon the sender. Farewell."

– SENECA

Introduction

Maybe you've stumbled upon a smart quote by an ancient Stoic philosopher or you've read an article that shared some inspiring Stoic ideas. Maybe you've been told about that helpful and flourishing old philosophy by a friend or you've already studied a book or two about Stoicism. Or maybe, although chances are very low, you've never even heard about it before.

However, encountering Stoicism in one way or another is the easy part. Understanding and explaining exactly what it is, though, is the tricky part. Recognizing and seeing exactly how it's relevant today and how it can help you, is the challenging part. Fully grasping it and putting it into practice, is the ambitious part—that's where the gold is hidden.

What the Stoics taught and practiced in the era of gladiators fighting for their lives and Romans socializing in steaming baths is still remarkably applicable in the era of *Game of Thrones* and Facebook. The wisdom of this ancient philosophy is timeless, and its value in the quest for a happy and meaningful life is undeniable.

With this book, you're holding the treasure map in your hands. It introduces you to the leading philosophers. It gives you an easy to understand overview of the philosophy. It teaches you the core principles. It provides you with 55 Stoic Practices and helpful hints for the application in your challenging life. And most importantly, it shows you how to translate it from book page to action in the real world.

Cool! But how does a twenty-something know how to write the Stoic treasure map for the good life? Fair enough, I'd be wondering about that too. After many years of school and university, I was sick of reading academic books and papers and learning about stuff that didn't really teach me anything of real life value. So, literally the day after handing in my final paper, I left the country and started my seven months long travel around the world. I wanted to get away, see places and other cultures, but mainly I wanted to get to know myself so I'd know what I wanted to do with my life when I got back. That last part did *not* work out; however, I *did* figure out something else instead: "I somehow must have missed the class on how to live?!"

In fifteen and a half years of schooling, I learned math, physics, chemistry, biology, and a bunch of other stuff, except how to deal with challenging situations? How to face my fears and struggles? What to do about my depressive feelings? How to deal effectively with the death of my friend? What to do with my anger? How to be more confident? Nope, I must have missed all those classes. That, by the way, is exactly what schools of philosophy were all about in the ancient world, they taught you how to live. And even though these schools don't exist anymore, you and I and most people are in as much need of a philosophy that teaches us how to live as we ever were.

Long story short, I decided to invest in myself and learn how to live well. From all the wisdom I devoured in the following years, Stoic philosophy helped me the most, even though it didn't start on good terms. Before I knew much (anything) about the philosophy, I thought this must be the most boring thing on earth. I mean, after all, it's called *Stoicism* and not "Supermanism" or something else that would indicate it's worth studying.

I gave it a shot anyway, got hooked, and since then I've been a voracious student and practitioner of Stoic philosophy. And even though I've read and reread countless books, I've always lacked a source that provides a simple overview and explains what exactly Stoicism is. So I wrote this massive article that should do exactly that: Give an overview of the philosophy and say what it's all about. Fortunately, many people loved the article and found it immensely helpful—so much, actually, that someone stole the exact content and sold it as his book. That did not only test my personal Stoic mindset, but all the five-star reviews it got told me that people really *want* to learn about this philosophy.

So here I am, passionately writing about what would have saved me countless weeks of research and would have provided so much sought-after and desperately needed wisdom from this exemplary philosophy. I'm positive that this book will contribute to the modern Stoic literature and, most importantly, that it will serve you well on your quest for the good life. Because that's really what Stoicism helps you with: living a great life.

Whatever you're going through, there's advice from the Stoics that can help. Despite the philosophy's age, its wisdom often feels surprisingly modern and fresh. It can help you build stamina and strength for your challenging life. It can help you become emotionally resilient so you'll neither get jerked around by outside events nor will others be able to push your buttons. It can teach you to handle yourself and stay calm in the midst of a storm. It can help you make decisions and therefore drastically simplify everyday living.

"He who studies with a philosopher," Seneca says, "should take away with him some one good thing every day: he should daily return home a sounder man, or in the way to become sounder." Practicing Stoicism helps you improve yourself as a person; it teaches you to mindfully live by a set of desirable values such as courage, patience, self-discipline, serenity, perseverance, forgiveness, kindness, and humility. Its many anchors offer security and guidance and will level up your confidence.

And *you* can get that too. In fact, Stoic philosophy made the good life a reachable goal for everybody, cutting through social classes—whether you're rich or poor, healthy or sick, well-educated or not, it makes no difference to your ability to live the good life. The Stoics were living proof that it's possible for someone to be exiled to a desert island and still be happier than someone living in a palace. They understood very well that there's only a loose connection between external circumstances and our happiness.

In Stoicism, what you *do* with the given circumstances matters much more. Stoics recognized that the good life depends on the cultivation of one's character, on one's choices and actions rather than on what happens in the uncontrollable world around us. This, my fellow Stoic student, is at the root of a tough and at the same time highly attractive aspect of Stoicism—it makes us responsible and deprives us of any excuses for not living the best life possible.

You and I, we're responsible for our own flourishing. We're responsible for not letting our happiness depend on external circumstances—we shouldn't let the rain, annoying strangers, or a leaking washing machine decide upon our wellbeing. Otherwise, we become helpless victims of life circumstances out of hand. As a Stoic student, you learn that only *you* can ruin your life and only *you* can refuse to let your inner self be conquered by whatever nasty challenge life throws at you.

So, Stoicism teaches us to live by a set of values that contribute to emotional resilience, calm confidence, and a clear direction in life. Just like an old reliable walking stick, it's a guide to life based on reason rather than faith, a guide that supports us in the pursuit of self-mastery, perseverance, and wisdom. Stoicism makes us better human beings and teaches us how to excel in life.

Its powerful psychological techniques are almost identical to the ones that are now proven to be effective by research in the scientific study called Positive Psychology. I am not accusing the researchers of theft, but the exercises discussed in Positive Psychology look suspiciously similar to the ones the Stoics used over two thousand years ago. The fact that modern research often goes hand in hand with what the Stoics taught makes the philosophy even more appealing. On top of that, Stoicism isn't rigid, but open and looking for the truth. As a Latin saying goes: "Zeno [founder of Stoicism] is our friend but truth is an even greater friend."

If we look around, we see countless people who pursued their dreams of a golden mansion, a Porsche 911, and a six-figure job, and yet they're not happier than before with the moldy flat, the rusty old car, and the cheap job. They're living by a formula that looks something like this: If you work hard, you'll be successful, and once you're successful, *then* you'll be happy. Or, if I finish/get/achieve such and such, *then* I'll be happy. The only problem? This formula is broken. And after following this formula for years, these people are wondering: *Is this really all life has to offer?*

No, it's not. The point is, many people don't get any happier when they grow older, they don't improve whatsoever. They mindlessly stroll through life lacking clear direction, repeatedly make the same mistakes, and won't be any closer to a happy and meaningful life in their eighties than they were in their twenties.

It should really be a no-brainer for many of us to adopt a philosophy of life that offers guidance, direction, and a larger meaning to life. Without that compass, there's the risk that despite all our well-intentioned actions, we'll run in circles, chase worthless things, and end up living an unfulfilling life full of emotional suffering, regrets, and frustration. And since it doesn't take much effort to give Stoicism a chance as your guiding philosophy of life, there's really nothing to lose and much to gain.

The promise of this book is really the promise of Stoic philosophy: It teaches how to live a supremely happy and smoothly flowing life and how to retain that even in the face of adversity. It prepares you to be ready for anything, like a tower of strength—unshakable, deep-rooted, emotionally resilient, and surprisingly calm and mindful even in the midst of a hellfire.

Stoicism can improve your life in good times, but it's in bad times when its efficacy becomes most apparent. It can be the light showing you the way through pitch-black depressive moments. It holds your hand when you need confidence to minimize emotional suffering by taming the bad guys like anger, fear, and grief. It can be your stepping stool to reach that tranquility you need when you're knee-deep in trouble. It can be your strong backbone when you need to act courageously even if you're shaking like a leaf. It can be the clown that wakes you up and casts a smile on your face when you need it the most.

In short, Stoicism not only shows you the way but also hands you the key to the good life. All you need to do is walk the path, turn the key, and enter. So, Stoic teacher Epictetus asks, "How long are you going to wait?"

"How long are you going to wait before you demand the best of yourself?" You're no longer a child but a full-grown person, and yet you procrastinate, Epictetus reminds himself. "You will not notice that you are making no progress but you will live and die as someone quite ordinary." From now on, he warns himself, and all of us, to live like a mature human being and never set aside what you think is best to do. And whenever you encounter anything difficult, remember that the contest is now, you are at the Olympics, you cannot wait any longer.

We don't have the luxury of postponing our training, because unlike the Olympic Games, the contest we participate in every day—life—has already begun. Life is right now, it's about time to start our training.

Training in Stoicism is a bit like surfing—little theory and lots of practice. Right now, you can't wait to get started and you imagine yourself standing on the surfboard hitting wave after wave, having the time of your life . . . *wait*, I have to stop you right there. Because in your first surf lesson, you get to learn some theoretical aspects of surfing too. On the dry land, you practice how to paddle, pop up, and stand on the board. In other words, the first part feels annoying—you just wanted to surf, you didn't sign up for that dry theory lesson.

Surprisingly quickly you make it through the theory part and you get to enter the water, flush out the sandy mouth, and start your practice. In the water, you quickly realize that it's not so easy, and the theory part was actually necessary. It's the same with Stoicism. You'll get to hit the waves, but if you want to hit them successfully and not give up after the first few (many) nosedives, you first need to understand some of the theory behind surfing . . . ahem, Stoicism.

I sought to organize this book and present the ancient wisdom in an accessible, digestible, and highly functional way. In the first part, you'll learn about the promise of the philosophy, its history, main philosophers, and about the core principles presented as the Stoic Happiness Triangle. Study that triangle and you're able to explain the philosophy to a five-year-old. The second part is all about hitting the waves; it's crammed with practical advice and exercises for everyday living.

My ultimate aim of this direct and straightforward approach to Stoicism is to help you live a better life. I believe we can all become a little wiser and happier by practicing this wonderful philosophy.

It's time to dive in.

PART 1

What is Stoicism?

"If it is not right, do not do it, if it is not true, do not say it."
– MARCUS AURELIUS

Chapter 1

The Promise of Stoic Philosophy

No tree becomes deep-rooted and sturdy unless strong winds blow against it. This shaking and pulling is what makes the tree tighten its grip and plant its roots more securely; the fragile trees are those grown in a sunny valley. "Why then," asks Seneca, "do you wonder that good men are shaken in order that they may grow strong?" Just like for the trees, heavy rain and strong winds are to the advantage of good people, it's how they may grow calm, disciplined, humble, and strong.

Just like the tree must tighten its grip not to fall down with every breeze, we must strengthen our position if we don't want to be swept off our feet by every trifle. This is what Stoic philosophy is here for—it will make you stronger and let the same rain and wind appear lighter and keep you on your feet at all times. In other words, it will prepare you to deal more effectively with whatever stormy weather life throws at you.

From wrestling philosophers to emotional wolves, this first chapter covers all you need to know about the promise of Stoic philosophy, or why you should get into Stoicism.

Warning: This book will contain some scary words like *eudaimonia*, *areté*, or *virtue*. Their unknown looks will make you want to turn the page, so brace yourself and stand strong. Despite the resistance, it will pay off to hang in there and you might even add them to your everyday vocabulary. And hey, this wouldn't be ancient philosophy without at least some scary words.

Practice the Art of Living: Become a Warrior-Philosopher

"First say to yourself what you would be;

and then do what you have to do."

– EPICTETUS

How to live a good life? This classic philosophic question stands at the origin of the primary concern of Stoic philosophy: How to live one's life, or "the art of living." Stoic teacher Epictetus compared philosophy to artisans: As wood is to the carpenter, and bronze to the sculptor, so are our own lives the proper material in the art of living. Philosophy is not reserved for wise old men, it's an essential craft for everybody who wants to learn how to live (and die) well. Every life situation presents a blank canvas or a block of marble that we can sculpt and train on, so that over a lifetime we can master our craft. That's basically what Stoicism does, it teaches us how to excel in life, it prepares us to face adversity calmly, and simply helps us sculpt and enjoy a good life.

What makes someone good at living? According to Epictetus, it's neither wealth, nor high-office, nor being a commander. There must be something else. Just like someone who wants to be good at handwriting must practice and know a lot about handwriting, or someone who wants to be good in music must study music, someone who wants to be good at living, therefore, must have good knowledge of how to live. Makes sense, right? Seneca, another important Stoic philosopher we'll get to know in Chapter 2, said that "[the philosopher] is the one who knows the fundamental thing: how to live."

A "philosopher" literally translates from the Greek into a "lover of wisdom," someone who *loves* to learn how to live, someone who *wants* to attain practical wisdom concerning how to actually live their life. As Epictetus told us before, if we want to become good at living, we must attain knowledge on how to live. This might surprise you, but philosophy is really a matter of *practice*, learning how to sculpt our lives. Thinking and philosophizing about the blank block of marble won't teach us how to skillfully use chisel and mallet. The Stoics were particularly concerned with *applying* philosophy to everyday life. They saw themselves as veritable *warriors of the mind* and thought the primary reason to study philosophy was to put it into practice.

This is a great comparison made by author Donald Robertson in his book *The Philosophy of Cognitive Behavioural Therapy*. He said that in ancient times, the ideal philosopher was a veritable *warrior* of the mind, but in modern times, "the philosopher has become something more bookish, not a warrior, but a mere *librarian* of the mind." Think of the old grey philosopher teacher. So we want to be *warriors* and what matters most is not our ability to recite Stoic principles, but to actually *live* them out in the real world. As Epictetus asked his students, "If you didn't learn

13

these things in order to demonstrate them in practice, what did you learn them for?" He continued that they (his students) were not hungry and courageous enough to go out in the real world and demonstrate the theory in practice, "Which is why I would like to escape to Rome to see my favorite wrestler in action, he, at least, puts policy into practice."

True philosophy is a matter of little theory and a lot of practice, like wrestling in the ancient and surfing in the modern world. Remember, in surfing, we get to practice in the water after a quick theory part on the beach. Heavy waves are better teachers than heavy school books. And Stoicism demands exactly that, to go out there in the real world and vigorously apply what we've learned in the classroom. Our lives offer the perfect training ground for daily practice with its uncountable green waves and blank marble blocks.

This practical "art of living" dimension of Stoicism holds two main promises: First, it teaches how to live a happy and smoothly flowing life, and second, it teaches you how to stay emotionally resilient to retain that happy and smoothly flowing life even in the face of adversity. Let's dive into the first promise and tackle the first of the scary words: *eudaimonia*.

Promise #1: Eudaimonia

> "Dig within. Within is the wellspring of Good; and it is always ready to bubble up, if you just dig."
>
> – MARCUS AURELIUS

Imagine the best version of yourself. Look inside, do you see and know who that highest version of you is, the one who acts right in all situations, the one who makes no mistakes and seems unbeatable? If you're anything like me and have been trying to improve yourself, then you probably know this ideal version of yourself. Well, in Greek, this best version would be the inner *daimon*, an inner spirit or divine spark. For the Stoics and all other schools of ancient philosophy, the ultimate goal of life was *eudaimonia*, to become good (*eu*) with your inner daimon. (Not to be confused with *demon*, which is a bad spirit.)

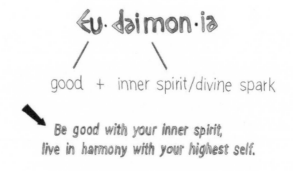

Eu·dai mon·ia

good + inner spirit/divine spark

Be good with your inner spirit,
live in harmony with your highest self.

The Stoics believed that nature *wants* us to become that highest version of ourselves. This is why the inner daimon (or divine spark) has been planted within all of us like a seed, so that we have it in our natural potential to become that highest version of ourselves. In other words, it's our *nature* to complete what's been started with that divine seed and bring our human potential to life. To become good with our inner daimon, to live in harmony with our ideal self is, therefore, to get as close as possible to that high potential self.

We should close the gap between *who we're capable of being* (our ideal self) and *who we actually are* in that moment. How can we do that? The Stoics had a word for that too: *areté*. In short, *areté* directly translates as "virtue" or "excellence," but it has a profounder meaning—something like "expressing the highest version of yourself in every moment." We'll dive deeper into that in Chapter 3, but you can already see that Stoicism deals with your moment-to-moment actions and with living as close as possible to your ideal self.

The Stoics' overarching goal was eudaimonia; to be good with your inner daimon, to live in harmony with your ideal self, to express your highest version of yourself in every moment. But what does that mean exactly? The most common translation of the Greek word eudaimonia is *happiness*. The translations "flourishing" or "thriving," however, capture the original meaning better because they indicate a form of continuing action—you can only be good with your daimon when your moment-to-moment actions are in harmony with your ideal self. You *flourish* at living well, and only *as a consequence* you'll feel happy.

Eudaimonia refers more to the overall quality of someone's life rather than a temporary mood such as happiness. It's a condition in which a person is thriving and living optimally well and supremely happy. As Zeno, the founder of Stoicism, puts it, "happiness is a smoothly flowing life." This entails that your life *generally* flows smoothly. Let's conclude that eudaimonia is a happy and smoothly flowing life that comes from thriving at bringing our moment-to-moment actions into harmony with our highest self.

This promise of eudaimonia entails that we're armed with all we need to deal with whatever challenge we're facing in life. How else can we stay happy even when life gets tough? Because life is pretty easy when things are going well, it only gets arduous when things seem to turn against us, when we're facing difficulties and struggles. This brings us to the second promise of Stoicism: Philosophy trains us to be able to take on every obstacle in life with the right mindset so that life keeps on going smoothly.

Promise #2: Emotional Resilience

"To bear trials with a calm mind robs misfortune of its strength and burden."

– SENECA

"But what is philosophy?" asks Epictetus. "Doesn't it mean making preparation to meet the things that come upon us?" Yes, he says, philosophy prepares us to endure whatever happens. "Otherwise, it would be like the boxer leaving the ring because he took some punches." We could actually leave the ring without any consequences, but what if we'd abandon the pursuit of wisdom? "So, what should each of us say to every trial we face? This is what I've trained for, this is my discipline!" Hey, a boxer who gets punched in the face won't leave the ring, it's what he prepared for, it's *his* discipline. And the same is true for philosophers; just because life slaps, kicks, spits, and knocks us out doesn't mean we should give up and leave, it means we should get back up and keep on getting better. Such is life—it's like our boxing ring, punches and kicks are what we've signed up for, this is *our* discipline.

"Unharmed prosperity cannot endure a single blow," says Seneca, but a man who has gone through countless misfortunes "acquires a skin calloused by suffering." This man fights to the ground and carries on the fight even on his knees. He will never give up. The Stoics loved wrestling metaphors, so Marcus Aurelius similarly says, "The art of living is more like wrestling than dancing." We need to be prepared for sudden attacks. Nobody will ever tackle a dancer. The dancer will never get choked by adversity like a wrestler. So, as warrior-philosophers, we know that life will be challenging. Actually, we should even be rubbing our hands together and be looking forward to take some punches, knowing they will make us stronger and grow our skin thicker.

This is why we should *want* to engage and train in this fight they call life. Because we want to be strong, we want to live happy and smoothly flowing lives. We want to handle ourselves and our actions when life gets tough. We want to be a tower of strength, unshakable even at the peak of a rage attack. When others panic, we want to stay cool, well-considered, and be able to be the best we can be.

Practicing Stoicism helps us develop the tools to deal as effectively as humanly possible with whatever kicks and punches life throws at us. No matter what happens in our lives—we're ready for anything—we're prepared to take hooks and side-kicks, never give up, and make the best of it. This is the promise of Stoic philosophy. Yet, right now, if you get punched in the face, what's going to happen? You get emotional. Like everybody else, you either angrily fight back, or more likely, you start crying. The Stoics identified strong emotions as our ultimate weakness; especially when we let them dictate our behavior. They're toxic to eudaimonia and they're at the root of all human suffering. Unfortunately, according to the Stoics, most of us are enslaved to *passions*—strong negative emotions such as irrational fear, grief, or anger. This is why so many of us are miserable, we're far away from being a tower of strength, we're far away from being at good terms with our ideal self. Our passions cause us to act far beneath of what we're capable of.

If we want to be able to act like our ideal self, say the Stoics, we need to keep our emotions in check, we need to tame them so they won't get in the way of the good life. *No, thank you, I can't afford to panic right now.*

Tame Restricting Emotions (≠ Unemotional)

The promise of Stoic philosophy consists of both the supremely happy life (eudaimonia) and the preparation (ready for anything) to deal effectively with whatever life throws at us. Yet, we can only deal well with life's challenges when we're emotionally resilient and don't let our emotions jerk us around.

This is why we need to make progress toward taming and overcoming disturbing desires and emotions, so that, as Seneca puts it, the glitter of gold doesn't dazzle our eyes more than the flash of a sword, and that we can easily wave aside what other people crave and fear. This overcoming of one's emotions is sometimes called the Stoic "therapy of the passions" and might be the reason why Epictetus said: "The philosopher's school is a doctor's clinic."

Now, if we imagine a doctor's clinic to have a couch in it, then, with some cliché, we get a psychotherapist's room. Back in Epictetus' days, when you had problems with your mind or soul, you wouldn't see a shrink but a philosopher instead—they were the preferred *doctors of the mind.* The Stoics were great observers of the human mind and actually had many important psychological insights. They realized, for example, that what makes insults hurtful isn't their content, but our interpretation of those insults. They had a proper understanding of our mind and developed psychological techniques to prevent and deal with negative emotions (most techniques will be covered in the second part of this book).

Although Stoicism is a philosophy, it has a significant psychological component to it. Many of its beliefs, such as the goal to *thrive* as human beings, go hand in hand with modern research in Positive Psychology; this is something I find highly intriguing about Stoicism. It's beyond the scope of this book to look at the science behind the Stoic ideas, but if you happen to read a book on Positive Psychology, you'll see the consonance (Shawn Achor's *The Happiness Advantage* is a fantastic start.)

Just as there are ailments to the body, there are ailments to the mind; and the Stoics were well aware of that. They said it's *im*possible to flourish in life while being tormented by irrational emotions. Therefore, we need *apatheia*—the ability to overcome these interfering emotions. That's where the word "apathy" comes from, and it's a main reason for the classic misunderstanding that the Stoics were somehow *unemotional* or seeking to suppress their feelings. The other reason for that misunderstanding comes from the lowercase word *stoic* which means to "suck it up" or having a "stiff upper lip" and has absolutely nothing to do with the uppercase *Stoicism* this book is all about. Let's clear out this "Stoics are emotionless" misunderstanding right now.

Stoicism has nothing to do with suppressing or hiding one's emotions or being emotionless. Rather, it's about acknowledging our emotions, reflecting on what causes them, and learning to redirect them for our own good. In other words, it's more about *unslaving* ourselves from negative emotions, more like *taming* rather than getting rid of them.

Imagine strong emotions to be like your inner wolf—immensely powerful when let loose and able to pull you wherever it wants to. Emotions activate an *action tendency*—when you feel angry, for example, you have the tendency to clench your fists, shout, and throw stuff. Basically, when the inner wolf is angry, we let it take over, and then we blindly follow the action tendency and act out. What the Stoics found, however, is that we don't *need* to follow that tendency. We can train ourselves to act calmly despite feeling angry, act courageously despite feeling anxious, and going east despite the wolf pulling west.

Fortunately, we don't need to pretend the wolf isn't there, or even kill it (which isn't even possible). The Stoics want us to *tame* and learn to understand that wolf. Instead of letting it dictate our actions when it's angry, anxious, or hungry, we act calmly *despite* the anger. It can snarl and howl as much as it wants, we don't fear it and act as we choose to. The wolf doesn't have a say in our decisions any longer despite feeling the action tendency.

The goal isn't to eliminate all emotions, the goal is to *not* get overwhelmed by them despite their immense power. We feel the emotional wolf, but we keep on our path despite it pulling in another direction. "Okay, the wolf wants to freak out, but what would it help?" we say to ourselves. We rise above our emotions, we can hear it snarl, but we know we neither need to listen nor follow along.

The Stoics weren't unemotional people with hearts of stone. They acknowledged that desires and emotions are part of nature, but we have it within our power to rise above them and not get (too) disturbed by them. "No school has more goodness and gentleness; none has more love for human beings." says Seneca. "The goal which it assigns to us is to be useful, to help others, and to take care, not only of ourselves, but of everyone." The Stoics do care for their loved ones and fellow citizens; they just tame their emotions so they won't get irrationally overwhelmed by them. As Seneca puts it, there's nothing impressive about "putting up with that which one doesn't feel." Stoic author Donald Robertson explains it well: "A brave man isn't someone who doesn't experience any trace of fear whatsoever but someone who *acts courageously despite feeling anxiety*."

The Stoics want us to conquer our passions by becoming stronger than them and not by eliminating them. We will always feel the emerging emotional wolf, but we can train ourselves to recognize our *tendency* toward following along, and then deliberately *choose* whether to follow along or not. Stoicism will help us get less plagued by negative emotions and, at the same time, experience more positive emotions such as joy or tranquility. It's important to notice, however, that for the Stoics, these positive emotions are more like an *added bonus* than a motive by themselves. Let's look closer at tranquility as a by-product of practicing Stoicism.

Practice Stoicism and Become more Tranquil as a By-Product

It may come as a surprise, but Stoicism is a rather joyful philosophy of life. When you read the Stoics, you find cheerful and optimistic people fully enjoying what life has to offer. They weren't unemotional, they just recognized that strong emotions were their weakness and stood in their way to live as they're capable of.

Remember, the ultimate goal of life is eudaimonia—the happy and smoothly flowing life that comes from thriving at expressing your ideal version moment to moment to moment. And if you're enslaved to your emotional wolf, then you panic and follow your action tendencies that are way beneath of what you're capable of. That's why the Stoics want us to minimize the effects that strong emotions have on our lives, they want us to tame that wolf so that we can stay at the steering wheel at all times instead of letting the wolf take over whenever it wants to. Only then can we express our highest version and lastly live a happy and smoothly flowing life.

So when we're not enslaved to our emotions, we can express the highest version of ourselves in every moment. When we do that, there's simply no room for regret, fear, or insecurity. What results from this is a really helpful side effect—tranquility. In today's hectic world, it's what so many of us seek, to be able to stay calm, feel confident and secure, even in the midst of chaos. If we practice Stoicism, this is exactly what we get as a by-product. It's a by-product because it's not what the Stoics sought in the first place. They didn't seek tranquility, they sought eudaimonia, and tranquility came as an added (and welcomed) bonus. So it wouldn't really be consistent with Stoicism to practice it for tranquility's sake.

What's tranquility anyway? Seneca talks about the power of *euthymia* in his classic letters. He tells us that euthymia, which gets translated as tranquility, is all about knowing your path and walking that path. It's the feeling we get when we truly and utterly trust ourselves. You're confident that what you're doing is right, and you don't need to listen left and right for what others have to say. You don't need to second guess and compare yourself to others all the time. You trust in what you're doing because you're trying your best, and you're living accordingly to your values and know it's all you can do.

It's the calm confidence you feel when you're living your authentic self in integrity with your highest values. You get that peace of mind, says Seneca, because you have an unchanging standard you live by, not like the rest of mankind who "continually ebb and flow in their decisions, floating in a condition where they alternately reject things and seek them."

Stoicism will give you many anchors to hold yourself onto, so you can find your path and walk it assured. This will cause you to gain an inner tranquility, a calm confidence at all times, even when life gets tough and shows its meanest kicks and punches. Because you know why you do what you do. You have this inner security that you're doing the right thing and, come what may, you're steadfast like that tower of strength, and nothing can root you out.

Chapter 2

A Quick History Lesson

"I made a prosperous voyage when I suffered shipwreck."

– ZENO OF CITIUM

The year is around 320 BCE. A Phoenician merchant suffers shipwreck somewhere between Cyprus and the Greek mainland in the Mediterranean Sea. He just lost all his murex dye, a highly valuable purple-colored dye won from the murex sea snail, and with that all his wealth. We are talking about Zeno of Citium who, thanks to this shipwreck, should become the founder of Stoicism many years later.

Zeno's father was a merchant himself and used to return home from his travels with books purchased in the Greek city of Athens. This might be the reason why after the accident at sea, Zeno went to Athens, sat down in a book store, and read about the Athenian philosopher Socrates who taught around a century earlier. Zeno was so impressed that he asked the bookseller where men like this Socrates could be found. The bookseller pointed in the direction of Crates the Cynic, who was just walking by, and said, "Follow yonder man."

Indeed Zeno did follow Crates, who was a leading philosopher at the time, and became his pupil for years to come. Zeno was happy how his life took a turn and said, "It is well done of thee, Fortune, thus to drive me to philosophy." When looking back on the shipwreck time in his life, Zeno later commented, "I made a prosperous voyage when I suffered shipwreck."

Note: This intriguing shipwreck story was written down by Greek biographer Diogenes Laertius in his *Lives of Eminent Philosophers* around 150 years after Zeno's death. There are different versions of the story and the dates are inconsistent and contradictory. So we can't be sure whether this is the true story or just the most attractive founding story of Stoicism.

After studying with Crates for a time, Zeno chose to go and study with other leading philosophers, before he started his own philosophy several years later in around 301 BCE. Initially, his followers were called *Zenonians*, but came to be known as *Stoics* because Zeno gave his lectures in the *Stoa Poikilê*, the "Painted Porch," a famous colonnade decorated with paintings of historical battles, located in the Athenian city center. Stoicism was born. Unlike other schools of philosophy, the Stoics followed the example of their hero Socrates and met outside in the public, on this porch, where anyone could listen. So Stoic philosophy was for academic and ordinary people alike and therefore it was something like a "philosophy of the street."

As we've seen, Stoicism was not born out of nowhere, its founder Zeno and the early Stoics had been influenced by different philosophical schools and thinkers, especially by Socrates, the Cynics (like Crates), and by the Academics (followers of Plato). The Stoics adopted Socrates' question: How to live a good life? They focused on *applying* philosophy to everyday challenges, on developing a good character and becoming better human beings who excelled in life and cared about other people and nature itself. One thing the Stoics changed from the Cynics was that they abandoned the Cynic asceticism. Unlike the Cynics, the Stoics favored a lifestyle that allowed simple comforts. They argued that people should enjoy the good things in life without clinging to them. As Marcus Aurelius later said, "If you must live in a palace, then you can also live well in a palace." This allowance of comfort was something that made Stoicism more attractive back then, and certainly today too.

After the death of Zeno (who, by the way, was so admired by the Athenians that they built a bronze statue of him), Stoicism kept its place as a leading Athenian school of philosophy (alongside others) until 155 BCE, when something very important happened to ancient philosophy—the heads of Stoicism (Diogenes of Babylon) and other schools of philosophy were chosen as ambassadors to represent Athens in political negotiations with Rome, in Rome. While the negotiations are of little interest, the cultural impact this visit had is not. The Athenians gave packed lectures and sparked an interest in philosophy among the rather conservative Romans. Stoicism became a thriving school in Rome with all the famous Stoics whose writings serve as the major source of the philosophy today: Seneca, Musonius Rufus, Epictetus, and Marcus Aurelius (we'll get to them shortly.)

Stoicism was one of the most influential and respected schools of philosophy for nearly five subsequent centuries. It was practiced by the rich and the poor, the powerful and the sufferer alike, in the pursuit of the good life. However, after the deaths of its famous teachers—Musonius Rufus, Epictetus, and the Roman Emperor Marcus Aurelius—

Stoicism fell into a slump from which it has yet to recover. The lack of charismatic teachers and the rise of Christianity are the main reasons for the decline of the once so popular philosophy.

The idea of Stoicism, however, found its way into many writings of historical philosophers such as Descartes, Schopenhauer, and Thoreau. And it is finding its way back into the lives of ordinary people like you and me (no offense). This comeback of Stoicism can be traced back to Viktor Frankl's logotherapy and Albert Ellis' rational emotive behavior therapy, both of which were influenced by Stoic philosophy. In more recent years, authors such as Pierre Hadot, William Irvine, Donald Robertson, and especially Ryan Holiday have accelerated the return of Stoicism.

The Most Important Stoic Philosophers

Look around, you're in the middle of thousands of excited people swinging their flags, shouting and cheering madly for their favorite chariot racers down in the arena of the Circus Maximus—zoom out, go half a mile north, zoom in—Roar! Straight in front of you, a gladiator fighting a lion, on your right, a gladiator aiming his spear in your direction, left, a monstrous elephant sprinting at you! In these dramatic times, our main characters taught and practiced Stoic philosophy. Although philosophy is much less exciting than bloody battles in the Colosseum (where you just got smashed by an elephant), it's the philosophy that survived until today. For good reasons as you'll learn in the following chapters.

Now, we'll look at the four Roman Stoics whose writings and teachings survived for nearly two millennia and now build the foundation of Stoicism: Seneca, Musonius Rufus, Epictetus, and Marcus Aurelius. It's said that over a thousand books had been written on Stoic philosophy but only a handful survived—mainly the ones from these luminaries.

Luckily, these brilliant (but also flawed) men did not live in caves somewhere in the mountains, but all of them were fully engaged in society and worked hard to make the world a better place. You'll meet an incredible wealthy playwright and equivalent of the modern-day entrepreneur, you'll meet an early feminist, and a crippled slave who should become the main influence of the Roman Emperor and mightiest person in the world. To stay true to the name of this book, we'll only scratch the surface of these fascinating lives of the four most important Stoic philosophers.

Seneca the Younger (c. 4 BCE – 65 CE)

"If a man knows not which port he sails,

no wind is favorable."

– SENECA

The most controversial Stoic philosopher, Lucius Annaeus Seneca, mainly known as Seneca the Younger or simply Seneca, was born around the time of Jesus in Cordoba, Spain, and educated in Rome, Italy. He is renowned as one of the finest writers of antiquity and many of his essays and personal letters survived and serve as an important source of Stoic philosophy. These writings speak to us because he focused on the practical aspect of Stoicism, down to how to take a trip, how to deal with adversity and its provoked emotions such as grief or anger, how to handle oneself while committing suicide (which he was ordered to do), how to deal with wealth (which he only knew too well), and poverty.

Seneca lived an extraordinary life, a life that raises many questions when studied closely. Apart from his letters which are still read almost two millennia after his passing, he made it into the history books for many more reasons. He was a successful playwright. He got extremely wealthy thanks to smart financial undertakings (the modern-day entrepreneur and investor if you will). He was exiled for committing adultery with the emperor's niece to what he called the "barren and thorny rock" Corsica—which, by the way, is a popular holiday destination known for diverse and scenic landscapes. After eight years of exile, the emperor's new wife wanted Seneca as a tutor to her son Nero.

Once Nero became emperor, Seneca was promoted to his advisor and became one of the wealthiest people in the Roman Empire. According to author Nassim Taleb, who devoted a whole chapter to Seneca in his book *Antifragile*, "his fortune was three hundred million denarii (for a sense of equivalence, at about the same period in time, Judas got thirty denarii, the equivalent of a month's salary, to betray Jesus)." This extreme wealth while being a philosopher that promoted the indifference of external possessions is a reason why Seneca sometimes gets called a hypocrite. The other fact that raises questions is that he was the tutor and advisor of Emperor Nero, who was a self-indulgent and cruel ruler and had his mother and many other people killed. In 65 CE, Nero ordered Seneca to commit suicide because he was supposedly involved in a conspiracy against the Emperor.

Hypocrite or not, Seneca lived a turbulent life full of riches and power but also of philosophy and introspection (he understood well enough that he was imperfect). Stoicism remained a constant in his life and stamped his many helpful and inspirational letters that I'll quote liberally throughout this book.

Musonius Rufus (c. 30 CE – c. 100 CE)

"Since every man dies,

it is better to die with distinction than to live long."

– MUSONIUS RUFUS

The least known of the four great Roman Stoics, Gaius Musonius Rufus taught Stoic philosophy in his own school. We know little about his life and teachings because he didn't bother to write anything down. Fortunately, one of Musonius' pupils, Lucius, took notes during the lectures. Rufus advocated for a practical and lived philosophy. As he put it, "Just as there is no use in medical study unless it leads to the health of the human body, so there is no use to a philosophical doctrine unless it leads to the virtue of the human soul." He offered detailed advice on eating habits, sex life, how to dress properly, and how to behave toward one's parents. Besides thinking philosophy should be highly practical, he thought it should be universal. He argued that women and men alike can benefit from education and the study of philosophy.

Musonius Rufus was the most prominent Stoic teacher at the time and his influence in Rome was respectable. Too much so for tyrannical Emperor Nero that he exiled him to the Greek island Gyaros in 65 CE (and yes, exile was common in ancient Rome). Seneca's description of Corsica as a "barren and thorny rock" would have fitted much better to Gyaros, which really was (and still is) a desert-like island. After Nero's death in 68 CE, Musonius returned to Rome for seven years before he got exiled again. He died in around 100 CE and left behind not only the few lecture notes from Lucius, but also his most famous pupil, Epictetus, who as we'll see right now, became an influential Stoic teacher himself.

Epictetus (c. 55 CE – c. 135 CE)

"Don't explain your philosophy. Embody it."
– EPICTETUS

Epictetus was born a slave in Hierapolis (present-day Pamukkale in Turkey). His real name, if he had one, is unknown. Epictetus simply means "property" or "the thing that was bought." He was acquired by Epaphroditos, a wealthy freedman (that is, a former slave himself) who worked as a secretary to Emperor Nero in Rome, the place where Epictetus spent his youth. He was crippled in one leg either by birth or by an injury received from a former master. His new master Epaphroditos treated him well and allowed him to study Stoic philosophy under the most renowned teacher in Rome, Musonius Rufus.

Sometime after Nero's death in 68 CE, Epictetus was freed by his master—a common practice in Rome with intelligent and educated slaves. He started his own school and taught Stoic philosophy for nearly twenty-five years until the Emperor Domitian famously banished all philosophers from Rome. Epictetus fled and moved his school to Nicopolis, Greece, where he led a simple life with few possessions. After the assassination of Domitian, Stoicism regained its respectability and became popular among the Romans. Epictetus was the leading Stoic teacher at the time and could have moved back to Rome, but chose to stay in Nicopolis, where he died in around 135 CE. Despite its location, his school attracted students from all around the Roman Empire and taught them, among other things, how to retain dignity and tranquility even in the face of life's hardships.

Just like his own teacher Musonius Rufus, Epictetus didn't write anything down. Fortunately, there was again a geek among the students, Arrian, who radically took notes and wrote the famous *Discourses*—a series of extracts of Epictetus' lectures. (Now I'm the geek who is trying to organize all of Stoicism into a little book . . .) Arrian also compiled the short book *Enchiridion*, a summary of the most important principles of the *Discourses*. *Enchiridion* often gets translated as *Handbook*, but it literally means "ready at hand"—more like a dagger than a handbook, always ready to deal with life's challenges.

Marcus Aurelius (121 CE – 180 CE)

"It never ceases to amaze me:

we all love ourselves more than other people,

but care more about their opinion than our own."

– MARCUS AURELIUS

"Waste no more time arguing about what a good man should be. Be one." These words were written not by some slouch but by a rare example of a philosopher king and, at the time, most powerful man on earth—Marcus Aurelius, emperor of the legendary Roman Empire. He is the most well-known of all the Stoic philosophers and his *Meditations*, a series of 12 short books which he wrote entirely to himself (like a diary) as his own guidance and self-improvement, is considered one of the greatest works of philosophy of all time.

As a teenager, it's said Marcus not only enjoyed activities such as wrestling, boxing, and hunting, but also philosophy. He studied with different philosophers, one of which lent him a copy of Epictetus' *Discourses*, which became the single most important influence on him. When he was sixteen, Emperor Hadrian adopted Marcus' maternal uncle Antoninus, who in turn adopted Marcus (his real father died when he was younger). When Marcus entered palace life, his political power didn't go to his head (he didn't let it), neither as a co-emperor of his adoptive father nor as an emperor himself after Antoninus' death. For one thing, he exercised great restraint in his use of power and money. Furthermore, despite his interest in Stoic philosophy, he chose not to use his power to preach Stoicism and lecture his fellow Romans on the benefits of its practices. He was an exceptionally good emperor and ruled from 161 CE to his death in 180 CE and counts as the *last* of a succession of rulers known as the Five Good Emperors.

Chapter 3

The Stoic Happiness Triangle

"The blazing fire makes flames and brightness out of
everything thrown into it."
– MARCUS AURELIUS

Enough history, it's time to get to the heart of Stoicism. What did these fascinating philosophers believe and teach exactly? How did they plan to keep their promise of a supremely happy and smoothly flowing life? How can their principles prepare us to face whatever challenge life throws at us? And how can we tame our emotions and become an unshakable tower of strength? It's simple: you need to go out in the real world and train like a warrior-philosopher. But first, you need to know the rules to play by, you need to know what to fight for, and you need to know which direction to take. These are the core principles of Stoicism that you will learn in this part.

Now, you might think this should be fairly easy, *spit it out, what are the core principles?* I thought the same when I stumbled upon Stoicism the first time. I quickly got hooked, read quite a bit about it, and told friends about this cool philosophy. But when they wanted to know what it exactly was, then I failed miserably at explaining it. I realized that despite the many texts I'd read, I hardly knew anything about Stoicism, I couldn't even manage to explain it properly to friends.

As it turned out, it's not so easy to get a simple overview of the philosophy. The original texts—consisting of lecture notes, personal letters, and diary entries—don't offer a clear-cut answer like one out of a textbook. And even modern books lack foolproof explanations, I find. It's often a mix of fantastic Stoic ideas, which are definitely worth studying, but fail to bring across a simple overview to hold onto.

This is basically the idea behind the Stoic Happiness Triangle. It gives you a simple overview of the core principles of Stoicism. If you know the triangle, you know and are able to explain the most important aspects of what Stoicism is—even to a five-year-old. It's the best I could come up with to present Stoic philosophy in a simple and visual way, combining ancient and modern literature. I hope you'll find it helpful. And keep in mind that the Stoic Happiness Triangle is not what the Stoics taught per se, it's my visualization of their core teachings.

The Stoic Happiness Triangle in A Nutshell

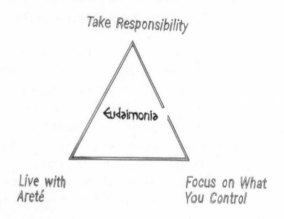

Eudaimonia: At the core of the triangle is eudaimonia—the ultimate goal of life all ancient philosophies agreed on. As touched in Chapter 1, this is the main promise of Stoic philosophy and it's about living a supremely happy and smoothly flowing life. It's about *thriving* in our lives. That's basically what we all want, to thrive and live happy lives, right? That's why it's at the core of the Stoic Happiness Triangle. Do you remember the Greek origin of the word? It means being on good terms (*eu*) with your inner *daimon*, your highest self. And how can we achieve this? By living with areté.

Live with Areté: Express your highest self in every moment. If we want to be on good terms with our highest self, we need to close the gap between what we're capable of and what we're actually doing. This is really about being your best version in the here and now. It's about using reason in our actions and living in harmony with deep values. This is obviously easier said than done, what supports this ambitious goal is to separate good from bad and focus on what we control.

Focus on What You Control: This is the most prominent principle in Stoicism. At all times, we need to focus on the things we control, and take the rest as it happens. What already *is* has to be accepted because it's beyond our power to undo it. What's beyond our power is ultimately not important for our flourishing. What's important for our flourishing is what we choose to *do* with the given external circumstances. So no matter the situation, it's always within our power to try to make the best with it, and to live in harmony with our ideal self.

Take Responsibility: Good and bad come solely from yourself. This follows the first two corners that say external things don't matter for the good life, so living with areté, which is within your control, is enough to flourish in life. Also, you're responsible for your life because every external event you don't control offers an area you can control, namely how you *choose to respond* to this event. This is crucial in Stoicism, it's not events that make us happy or miserable, but our interpretation of those events. This is when a tower of strength can be born—the moment you decide to give outside events no more power over you.

That's of course just the frame of the triangle, and we barely scratched the surface. In the coming pages, we'll look at each corner in detail with clarifying ideas and metaphors, and we'll get to know the villain that hinders so many of us from expressing our highest self moment to moment to moment. But first, let's remember the surfing analogy.

Up next is the highly important but not so fun theory part at the beginning of your first surf lesson. *Oh, there we go . . .* some wise guys run straight into the water, despite the warnings. It always happens. Here's the cool thing—once we're done here and you follow them in the water, you'll do better immediately because they lack the basics, and that's when you need to see their faces—priceless! However, some will come back earlier because they've realized they're lacking something or they've hurt themselves. Anyway, let's start without the runaways and you'll get in the water before you know it. On the sand, get set, go!

1. Live with Areté: Express Your Highest Self in Every Moment

"A good character is the only guarantee of everlasting,

carefree happiness."

– SENECA

The first corner of the Stoic Happiness Triangle is *Live with Areté*. The classic translation for this Greek word is "virtue" or "excellence." I prefer how Brian Johnson, the philosopher behind the website *optimize.me*, translates *areté*: "Expressing the highest version of yourself moment to moment to moment." Because of this deeper meaning of the word and because it apparently was one of the highest ideals of Greek culture, let's use the original word for the name of this first corner of the triangle. We'll necessarily use the common English translation *virtue* too, so keep that in mind.

The ultimate goal of Stoicism is positioned in the center of the triangle: *eu-daimon-ia*, to live a happy and smoothly flowing life. To achieve this goal, we need to be on good terms (*eu*) with our inner *daimon*, the highest version of ourselves, our natural inborn potential. In whatever you do, imagine there are two lines: the higher line indicating what you're *capable of* and the lower line what you're *actually* doing. Living with areté is about trying to reach the higher line and express what you're capable of in this very moment. That's actualizing the highest version of yourself, that's being on good terms with your inner daimon, that's when you achieve the happy and smoothly flowing life called eudaimonia.

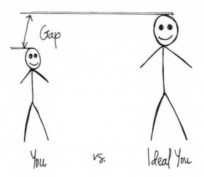

Now, this perfect actualization of our highest selves might not be too hard to express in single situations or in our imagination, but drag us out in the real world and we fail miserably. And that's ok, that's what we're here for, learning about ourselves and how to express our highest version moment to moment to moment. That's why we're trying to get better, that's why we're trying to improve our virtue. Think of areté or virtue as a form of wisdom or strength that helps you do the appropriate thing at all times, so that your actions are in harmony with your highest self—courageous, disciplined, and kind for example. Virtue is what helps you close the gap between what you're actually doing and what you're capable of. The bigger that gap, the further away you are from eudaimonia, and the worse off you are. Because somewhere in the darkness of the gap, they are lurking, the bad guys lead by regret, anxiety, and disillusionment.

Alright, virtue is about trying to be the best you can be in every moment. And if you're able to do that, then you'll have a good relationship with your highest self and will live a happy and smoothly flowing life. If you're unable to express the highest version of yourself, this will create space for

42

regret and anxiety to crawl out of the darkness and spread misery. This is highly important to know, but let's be honest, it doesn't help much yet. I mean, don't we all want to be the best we can be anyway? (I sure hope so.) Now, apart from *living with areté,* the Stoics used another stock phrase for the same goal of expressing the highest version of yourself: *living in agreement with nature.* Let's unravel that and see whether we're smarter afterward.

The Perfection of Our Natural Potential

The Stoics believed that nature *wants* us to thrive in life. This is why the inner daimon, our highest self, had been planted within all of us like a divine seed, so that we have it in our *natural potential* to become that highest version of ourselves. As Musonius Rufus said, we're all "*born* with an inclination toward virtue." In other words, it's our *nature* to complete what's been started with that divine seed and bring our human potential to life. So, a person's virtue depends on their excellence as a human being, on how well they perform their natural potential. To be virtuous, then, is to live as nature designed us to live. This is where the Stoic aphorism *living in agreement with nature* comes from.

Put simply, virtue is the same thing for all living beings—the perfection of their own nature. So, living with areté is basically to complete our nature. Without that completion, we lack something and our lives will remain unfulfilled. It's clear—if we don't live up to our innate potential, we'll never be fulfilled.

Let's look at an example in nature. The natural potential of a grape seed is to grow into a grapevine and bear grapes. So a grape seed *lives with areté* or *in agreement with nature* when it fulfills its natural potential by growing into a grapevine and producing grapes.

Just as it's enough for the good life for the grapevine to produce grapes, it's enough for us to express the highest version of ourselves moment to moment to moment. That's all it takes. Nothing external is required to get to the good life—no villa by the beach, no diamond rings, no porcelain plates, and generally nothing that hasn't been planted within as natural potential. And that's something that makes Stoicism so appealing. The potential to live the good life is within all of us—whether we're rich or poor, healthy or sick, model-like beautiful or other-kind of beautiful. All of us can get to the good life. But I'm getting ahead of myself, we'll learn more about the unimportance of external things in the second corner of the Stoic Happiness Triangle.

Your natural potential lies in your highest version of yourself. Yet there's more. The Stoics argued that the most significant difference with other animals is the human's ability to use *reason*. Stoic teacher Epictetus explained that what separates us from wild beasts and sheep is our *rational* element and not the naked skin, weaker bones, or missing tails. We negate our very humanity and fall to the state of a sheep when we let our *actions* become impulsive and inconsiderate. He asked, "When our actions are combative, mischievous, angry, and rude, do we not fall away and become wild beasts?"

Epictetus' point is that our ability to use reason is at the core of our natural potential we need to fulfil, and it shows best in our actions, by expressing it moment to moment to moment. On one hand, the ability to use reason is our most precious gift and, if we live by it, we'll have a happy and smoothly flowing life—like a grapevine that produces grapes. On the other hand, it's our heaviest burden, because if we *fail* to live by it, we fall to the level of a beast, negate our humanity, and won't live a happy life—much like a grapevine that fails to produce edible grapes.

For the Stoics, then, it's *reason*able to always try to be the best you can be. We all have this seed of reason, this seed of our highest self, planted within. And therefore, we've got the potential to live a virtuous life—that is, a life led by reason and expressing our ideal self. This expression shows as generally honorable and praiseworthy actions that benefit ourselves and others. As learned earlier, virtue is for all living beings the perfection of their own nature; in the case of humans, then, virtue is the *perfection of reason.* Put differently, living with areté is the perfection of expressing our highest self in every moment. Remember, living with areté, virtue, reason, and in agreement with nature are all different expressions for the same goal.

In Stoic philosophy, it's clear that the perfection of reason not only included *rational,* but also *social* actions in the form of duties to our fellow men, such as honoring our parents, being agreeable to our friends, and being interested in the wellbeing of mankind. As rational *and* social creatures, we should therefore apply reason and express our highest selves to three main areas of life:

- **Our own mind**: As human beings with the ability of reasonable thinking, we should consider our actions rationally and wisely, and at all times try to be the best we can be.
- **With other people:** As social beings who naturally care for each other, we should try to live

harmoniously with others and contribute to the wellbeing of mankind.

- **In the universe:** As citizens of the vast cosmos, we should try to live harmoniously with nature, calmly accept events that happen to us, and try to respond wisely.

I know, this whole areté, virtue, reason, and fulfilling our nature idea is highly abstract and it's difficult to have a clear understanding of how this looks like in practice. Luckily, the Stoics used a more graspable classification of virtue that divided it into four desirable character traits known as the four *cardinal virtues*. Before we look at them, though, let's quickly look at the Stoic *Sage*, the hypothetical ideal the Stoics used to portray the perfectly wise and good person—the Adonis of character, if you will.

You might have been wondering, *is it even possible to be the best we can be in every moment?* No, it's not. This is why the Stoics used the Sage as an ideal, because there are no perfect humans. And we don't need to be perfect for the Stoics, but we can at least try to be as good as possible. This is why they contemplated the Sage, they wanted to be as good as possible and just like the Sage attain perfect eudaimonia. "He lives in total harmony with himself, the rest of mankind, and Nature as a whole," describes Donald Robertson, "because he follows reason and accepts his fate graciously, insofar as it is beyond his control. He has risen above irrational desires and emotions, to achieve peace of mind. His character is absolutely praiseworthy, honourable and beautiful."

No wonder the Sage is a hypothetical ideal, but the Stoics say it's beneficial to have someone to look up to and compare ourselves against. The Sage makes it easier to imagine our ideal self and acts like a signpost showing the direction. Now, let's look at the four virtues with which we can try to deliver a Sage-like performance.

The Four Cardinal Virtues

You and me, we get closer to our common goal of the good life by making progress toward living with areté. Now, we can evaluate this progress in four broad character traits the Stoics adopted from the Socratic philosophy. They divided virtue into the four cardinal virtues of wisdom, justice, courage, and self-discipline. Living by these qualities makes a strong character and lets you take generally honorable and praiseworthy actions, just like the Sage. The opposite immoral and wicked character traits are known as the four *cardinal vices*. *Kakia* is the Greek word that opposes areté and it makes a weak character that shows as shameful and ignorant behavior. Let us look at all of them, one by one:

Wisdom is about understanding how to act and feel appropriately. Wisdom includes excellent deliberation, healthy judgment, perspective, and good sense. It opposes the vice of folly or thoughtlessness.

Justice is about knowing how to act and feel well in our relationships with others. Justice includes good-heartedness, integrity, public service, and fairness. It opposes the vice of wrongdoing or injustice.

Courage is about knowing how to act and feel correctly when facing fearful situations. Courage includes bravery, perseverance, honesty, and confidence. It opposes the vice of cowardice.

Self-Discipline (or temperance) is about knowing how to act and feel right, despite emotions such as strong desire, inner resistance, or lust. Self-discipline includes orderliness, self-control, forgiveness, and humility. It opposes the vice of excess.

These are definitely character traits worth striving for, right? If you're anything like me, these make intuitive sense and we all, even across different religions and cultures, value these same traits in people among us and ourselves. When you read through those, you might think you're good at *justice* because you always treat others with exceptional fairness, but you're not so good at *self-discipline* because you often struggle with sticking to that *one* glass of Rioja. Now, even though it makes perfect sense to say that you're better at some of them and worse at others, for the Stoics, it's always the whole package that counts. Virtue is an all-or-nothing package.

The Stoics offered an analogy to clear things up: Someone can be a poet, an orator, *and* a general, but at the same time he's still only *one* individual. And so too are the virtues unified in one but can be applied to different areas of action. So, this person can be an excellent poet, an okay orator, and a lousy general, but what matters is the person as a whole and not the single actions in their respective areas. And if we think about it, this all-or-nothing package makes sense. After all, we don't want to call a highly self-disciplined and courageous bank robber a virtuous person.

Perfect virtue is an ideal only the Sage can reach, but it's encouraging to see that what matters is you as a whole being. You can grow and ripen as a whole person and it doesn't matter whether someone observes your virtuous actions or not, making progress and trying to be the best you can be is enough. So virtue is essentially one form of *practical* wisdom: to *know* what's the appropriate thing to do, and to actually *do* it. And keep in mind that just like a grapevine won't produce perfect grapes in its first years, and will continue to have some sour grapes even in its prime, you too will get better if you try to be your best but you'll also continue to show some flaws. This imperfection is perfectly natural and something the Stoics observed in their own lives.

Here's an example from Seneca: "When the light has been taken away and my wife has fallen silent, aware as she is of my habit, I examine my entire day, going through what I have done and said." Seneca pleaded his case at his own court every night and shared some examples in his letter *On Anger*. My favorite story is when at some event he got angry because he was not seated in a place of honor he thought he deserved. He spent the evening being angry with the host who seated him and with the guests who were seated above him. "You lunatic," he wrote in his journal, "what difference does it make what part of the couch you put your weight on?"

The point is, nobody will ever be perfect in all their actions and, as long as we're trying our best, this doesn't matter. The world isn't black and white, we can't always tell what the right thing to do is, but we can always try to act with our best intention. And that's what I find is the easiest way to understand living with areté—at all times, try to be the best you can be, try to choose the appropriate action/response, and simply try to be a good person with concern for others and nature as a whole. In other words, develop your character. And that's what we'll look at after an important side note.

Attention (literally): If we want to be the best we can be in every situation, if we want to live with areté, then we need to be aware of our every step. Today, we call this "mindfulness," the Stoics used the term "attention" (*prosochê*). In the words of Marcus Aurelius, we should pay "vigorous attention . . . to the performance of the task in hand with precise analysis, with unaffected dignity, with human sympathy, with dispassionate justice." We can achieve such a mind free of other thoughts by performing "each action as if it were the last of your life."

Imagine you're walking barefoot along the beach when suddenly a section is full of bits of broken glass. Now you walk very cautiously and watch every step like a hawk so you don't hurt yourself—*that's* the attention the Stoics want us to pay to every action. This focused attention and continuous self-observation is necessary if we actively want to align our actions with virtue, for how could we make sure we act virtuously if we weren't even aware of our actions? As we let our thoughts drift away, our actions become *mindless,* we stumble into folly, and give away our best chance for eudaimonia as we're far off from being our best in this very moment. This will happen countless times, but that's when mindfulness is needed most. "A consciousness of wrongdoing is the first step to salvation," Seneca says. "You have to catch yourself doing it before you can correct it." Just like he did when he realized what a lunatic he was for getting angry at others about his seating. Without such consciousness, our actions become impulsive, automatic, and random—exactly the opposite of what we want.

"Attention (*prosochê*) is the fundamental Stoic spiritual attitude," explains author Pierre Hadot. "It is a continuous vigilance and presence of mind, self-consciousness which never sleeps, and a constant tension of the spirit. Thanks to this attitude, the philosopher is fully aware of what he does at each instant, and he *wills* his actions fully." Even if this consciousness which never sleeps is the Stoic's goal, Epictetus said that it's not possible to be faultless, but we can try and "we must be content if by never remitting this attention we shall escape at least a few errors."

Character Beats Beauty

"Lay aside the senator's dress, and put on rags and appear in that character." No matter which role you happen to play in society, no matter if you wear a suit and tie or socks and sandals, Epictetus is pointing out that what matters is your core, your character. The only way to recognize a true Stoic, then, is by their character.

Think about someone you know who has a character of granite. *Bruno* comes to my mind. Bruno was one of my early soccer coaches. He was dependable, trustworthy, and most importantly, he was consistent in his actions. He was fair and honest not only when it was convenient, but always. He was a man solid as a rock with a pinch of fantastic humor. I am sure you can think of a Bruno in your own life and it becomes clear why Stoicism values a person's character so greatly.

"Character beats beauty," I once wrote in an article. This is probably not true for our times, which will be referred to as the *beauty mania epoch* in history books, but it's definitely true in Stoic philosophy. The Stoics would go a step further and claim that "character beats not only beauty, but also riches, power, and yeah, even the Joker." Being a person of virtue really means to excel at one's character and always trying to do your best and what's generally honorable and praiseworthy. Virtue really is the highest good in Stoicism and living by it will ultimately shape you into a genuinely good person. And that will come with extra bonuses. Let me explain.

Let's go back to Bruno. Do you think his consistently fair and honest actions went unnoticed? No! He got promoted as a coach many times and became one of the most important figures at the club. As far as I know, everyone loved and appreciated him. His trustworthy and steadfast character brought him many bonuses. Just to mention a few: love and admiration from his players, respect and power at the club, and so on. And thanks to these bonuses, Bruno most certainly experienced feelings of joy and worthiness.

And so it can be in our lives too. When we act bravely, honestly, and just, then we might get some good feelings in return. When you raise your voice against Jimmy the bully, the victim might thank you for it and you'll be proud as a consequence. When you tell your parents the truth about that joint, you might feel relieved. When you persevere in your job search, you'll feel happy once you get accepted.

For the Stoics, it's important that these positive feelings should not be the primary motives of our virtuous actions. The positive feelings should be looked at as *added bonuses*. Virtue must absolutely be its own reward for at least two reasons:

1. The added bonus (e.g., feeling of joy) is not under our control.
2. The added bonus could be caused by other *non-*virtuous actions.

You should act virtuously because it's the right thing to do and not because it will benefit you in some way or another. Help the bullied girl because it's the appropriate thing to do and not because you'll feel great afterward and you'll get a chance for a date. The added bonuses are uncertain and not under your control. You only control your action and not what happens afterward. Yes, you might feel good about helping her. Yes, you might get her number. But also, you might get slapped in the face by the bully. And you might get ignored by the girl. So, a Stoic should be willing to act with courage *despite* his feelings pulling him back rather than *because* of possible future benefits.

Marcus Aurelius describes this elegantly in his *Meditations*. He distinguishes between three types of people. The first type of people, after doing a deed of kindness to another, is quickly to demand the favor in return. The second type of people are not so quick to ask for a return of the favor, but privately think of the other as their debtor. The third type of people are just "like the vine which has produced grapes and looks for nothing else once it has borne its own fruit." Like a horse after its race or a bee after producing honey, this third type ask for nothing but pass on to the next action, "just as the vine passes on to bear grapes again in due season." It's in our *nature* to do good to others, and we should do it for its own sake.

The Stoic Love of Mankind: Act for the Common Welfare

We're social creatures with a natural affection toward other people. Stoic philosophy is full of goodness, gentleness, love for human beings, and attention to the common good, says Seneca. The goal is to be useful, to help others, and to take care of ourselves and everybody else.

The Stoics nurtured this idea that we should be concerned with other people, wish them to flourish, and develop a sense of kinship with the rest of mankind: Treat even strangers and those who oppose us as relatives—brothers and sisters, aunts and uncles. We're all citizens of the same world. This shared affinity forms the basis for mutual love and friendship.

A person cannot attain anything good for himself, says Epictetus, "unless he contributes some service to the community." That's the nature of the social and rational animal we are. We're designed to live among other human beings, very much like bees, says Musonius Rufus: "A bee is not able to live alone: it perishes when isolated." And Marcus conveniently adds, "What brings no benefit to the hive brings none to the bee." Our actions must benefit the common welfare, or they won't benefit ourselves. We're like a massive organism: all depending on one another.

Our social duty is to feel a concern for all mankind, to work together, and to help each other. "For all that I do," says Marcus, "should be directed to this single end, the common benefit and harmony." We cannot express our highest selves without at the same time contributing to the common good. If we seek the very best in ourselves, we will actively care for the wellbeing of all other human beings. The best for others will be the best for you.

It's not that we are social in the sense that we like being around other people, it's in the deeper sense that we couldn't *exist* without the help of others. Therefore, when we do good to others, we actually benefit ourselves. Benefiting others is a form of virtue, and it ultimately benefits ourselves as virtue is its own reward. Now that you know doing good to others benefits yourself, you could selfishly do good to others. All for your own benefit.

And ultimately, it doesn't matter whether we do good to others for selfish or altruistic reasons, as long as the intention is to act for the common welfare. Remember the three types of people Marcus describes? The first always looking for a return, the second thinking that the other is his debtor, and the third, who is more like a grapevine, producing grapes and not looking for anything in return. It's his social duty to do good to others, and he won't look for anything in return.

Marcus says that fulfilling your social duties will simply give you the best chance at having a good life. That's the reward for acting for the common welfare, not gratitude, admiration, or sympathy—these are (uncertain) additional bonuses and shouldn't be the reason for your actions. So even Marcus Aurelius acted for the common good for a selfish reason—because he thought it would give him the best chance for a good life.

Living with areté and directing one's actions toward the common good is its own reward. This is our nature and it's ultimately our best chance to live a happy and smoothly flowing life. We must not look or wish for added bonuses such as admiration from others because they aren't within our control and can fade quickly. "But the wise person can lose nothing," Seneca argues, "their own goods are held firm, bound in virtue, which requires nothing from chance, and therefore can't be either increased or diminished."

Your character, stemming from your actions, is what you can rely on at all times. In Stoic philosophy, it's enough to try to express your highest self at all times, and direct your actions to the common good. That's all you can do. Marcus Aurelius beautifully reminds himself that a lamp shines until its fuel is fully spent. So why shouldn't his truth, justice, and self-control shine until he's extinguished? In that sense, let's light our lamps of virtue and let them shine by expressing our highest versions for as long as we may exist.

2. Focus on What You Control: Accept Whatever Happens and Make the Best Out of It

"What is it then to be properly educated? It is learning to apply our natural preconceptions to the right things according to Nature, and beyond that to separate the things that lie within our power from those that don't."

– EPICTETUS

"Of things some are in our power, and others are not." These are the very first words in Epictetus' *Enchiridion*. As we learned earlier, *Enchiridion* translates into *ready at hand*—like a dagger—and the separation between what is in our power and what is not, is something we should always have ready at hand, ready to help us deal with whatever life throws at us. The central teaching of Epictetus was that there are things which are up to us and things which aren't; we should always "make the best use of what is in our power, and take the rest as it happens." This idea is *the* cornerstone of Stoic philosophy, and therefore builds the second corner of our Stoic Happiness Triangle.

Imagine you hold in your hands a doll that looks just like you. Let's call it a *voodoo doll*. Beautiful. Now, you walk over to the window, open it, and throw your doll out into the street. You stay inside and hope for a sunny day with some lucky happenings. All of a sudden, life becomes an emotional roller coaster—without you having a say in it. Pug marks you, suit kicks you around, and Prius rolls you over. *Ugh . . .* life sucks! Now, nobody would actually do that with their own voodoo doll. Or would they? Isn't that exactly what many people do by worrying about stuff outside their own control? Right, that's the *root cause* of emotional suffering, to worry about outside events. Does Steven like me? Will I get that job? Why am I not taller/thinner/better looking? Handing power to things we have no direct control over causes emotional suffering. This is why the Stoics would tell us to take that imaginary voodoo doll back into our own hands, and let ourselves decide when to get kicked around and not. The point is, the Stoics want us to focus on what we control and let the pugs mark where they may.

What is it then that we have control over? Only a few things—our voluntary judgments and actions. We can decide what events mean to us and how we want to react to them (we'll look at our judgments more closely in the third corner of the Stoic Happiness Triangle.) And our actions, we can choose to align them with virtue, as discussed in the previous part. All else is not under our control. That's from the weather to other people and their actions to our health and body, and literally everything that happens around us.

Right, our body, for example, is not completely under our control. We can surely influence it with our behavior—we can lift weights, do some all-out sprints, and eat a broccoli a day—but this won't make our hips smaller, our shoulders wider, our nose straighter, or our eyes bluer. There are certain things that influence our body that we don't control, such as genes, early exposure, or injuries. The so-called Stoic *dichotomy of control*—some things are up to us, other things are not—is really about the recognition of *three* levels of influence we have over the world:

- **High influence:** Our choices in judgments and actions
- **Partial influence:** Health, wealth, relationships, and outcomes of our behaviors
- **No influence:** Weather, ethnicity, and most external circumstances

"This is wholly up to you—who is there to prevent you being good and sincere?" Marcus Aurelius often reminded himself of the power he was granted by nature—the power to choose his actions and craft his own character. He said people can't admire you for what's been granted to you by nature, but there are many other qualities to cultivate. "So display those virtues which are wholly in your own power— integrity, dignity, hard work, self-denial, contentment, frugality, kindness, independence, simplicity, discretion, magnanimity."

We are the only ones to stop ourselves from cultivating these qualities. It's within our power to prevent viciousness, curb our arrogance, stop lusting after fame, and control our temper. "Do you not see how many virtues you can display without any excuse of lack of talent or aptitude? Or does the fact that you have no inborn talent oblige you to grumble, toady, or blame?" No it does not! It's within our power to choose our behavior, even if everything else is not or only partially within our control.

Before we look at what's within our control in more detail, let's look at an example of it in practice. The Serenity Prayer, a prayer used by Alcoholics Anonymous and other recovery communities, is basically the idea applied in practice:

"God, grant me the Serenity to accept the things I cannot change, the Courage to change the things I can, and the Wisdom to know the difference."

Recovering addicts cannot change the abuse suffered in childhood, or maybe even before they were born. They cannot undo the choices they have made in the past; they cannot *un*snort the coke, *un*drink the booze, or *un*swallow the pills. They cannot undo the pain they have caused for themselves and others. But they can accept the past and try to change the now and the future by focusing on the choices they're making right now. And we can do the same by focusing on what we control—namely the choices we make every day—and taking the rest as it happens. For it is futile and therefore *foolish*, said Epictetus, to worry about things that are not up to us.

The Stoic Archer: Focus on the Process

As I'm Swiss, it's time for a Swiss legend. In the early fourteenth century, part of Switzerland was oppressed by the Habsburg emperors of Vienna. In one village, the cruel governor raised a pole in the market place, hung his feathered hat on top of it, and demanded everybody to bow respect before that hat. When William Tell and his son passed the place without bowing—either they didn't know or ignored it—Tell was forced to shoot an apple off his son's head with his crossbow. Luckily, he was an expert with the crossbow and hit the apple in a straight shot. He was arrested anyway for admitting that he'd prepared a second arrow to kill the governor in case he missed the apple and hit his son instead.

Thanks to a storm, Tell managed to flee from the boat that was supposed to bring him to the governor's castle for imprisonment. Knowing that he was facing a death sentence now, he hurried to the alley leading to the castle and waited in ambush. When the cruel governor and his followers came through the alley, William Tell leapt out and shot the governor with his second bolt straight through the heart, before he melted back into the woods. My fellow countryman's act of bravery sparked a rebellion and led to the free Swiss Confederacy—*hurray!*

Hundreds of years before Tell shot an apple off his son's head, the Stoics used the *archer metaphor* to explain their fundamental idea of focusing on what you control. Tell can draw his bow, close an eye, focus, aim, hold his breath, and finally pull the trigger. Now imagine the arrow to be in the air in slow motion. The arrow is out there, moving through the air toward the apple. It's out of control—Tell can't influence it anymore, he can only wait and see. An unexpected gust of wind could blow the arrow off course. A bird could fly directly in front of the arrow. The son could stoop down, or his mother could jump in and heroically take the hit.

The point is, Tell can try his best to the moment he pulls the trigger, but whether he hits the apple or the eye is not in his power. And the same is true for us in everyday life. We can choose our intentions and actions but the ultimate outcome depends on external variables beyond our control. This is the reason why the Stoics advised to focus on what we control, and let the rest happen as it will.

In modern times, we call this *process focus*—to focus on the process (under our control), instead of the desired outcome (not under our control). In archery, the desired outcome is to hit the target, but that's not where the focus should lie because it's beyond our control. It's smarter to focus on the process that will optimally lead to the desired outcome. The Stoics realized that the process will affect the outcome. The process is about our behavior, deliberate practice, and all that prepares us to shoot well.

Success, then, is defined by our effort to do everything that's within our power. Whether we hit the target or not, whether we win or lose, whether we drop some weight or not, ultimately does not matter. We succeed or fail already in the process. So the Stoic archer focuses on the process (preparing and shooting well); a possible positive outcome (hitting the target) won't arouse jubilation, and a possible negative outcome (missing the target) won't arouse despair. The Stoic archer succeeds in the process and is ready to take any outcome with equanimity and calm confidence, knowing they've tried their very best.

This focus on the process, focus on what you control idea, is a massive confidence booster. You know if you do your very best, you will succeed no matter what. It's all you can do. If you try your absolute best at your job, in your relationships, and for your health, then you'll always feel confident and at peace with yourself. This calm confidence or tranquility lies in knowing that you did whatever was in your power, because that's all you control. Even if things don't turn out well, you can derive satisfaction from knowing you've done your best. No need to justify bad results, there are just too many uncontrollable factors influencing the outcome.

It's only if you know you haven't done everything in your power that you will feel insecure and must justify yourself. That's the dark gap between what you're actually doing and what you're capable of doing, as discussed earlier. The Stoics highlighted that anxiety and inner disturbance come from wanting things out of our control. Epictetus, for example, said that it's foolish to want friends and relatives to live forever because it's not up to us. As seen before, the root cause of emotional suffering comes from worrying about things outside our control. This is why we should focus on the process; the process is fully under our control. And if we define success as giving our best in the process, then we cannot fail, feel calmly confident, and can accept any outcome with equanimity.

Stoic Acceptance: Enjoy the Ride or Get Dragged Along

"Suffering is our psychological resistance to what happens," explains Dan Millman in *The Way of the Peaceful Warrior.* Events can give us physical pain, but suffering and inner disturbance only come from resisting what is, from fighting with reality. We get angry at that driver that cut us off, we're unhappy with our exam grades, and we're desperate because the train is running late. If we look at those situations objectively, we recognize it's futile to fight with them, because we can't change or undo what already is. Yet, we fight with reality all the time and want it to be different. That driver shouldn't drive like that, my grades should be better, the train should be on time. We *must* have it our way, the way we want it, the way we expected it to be.

This is fighting with the Gods, says Epictetus, things are as they are because that's how it's meant to be. Our emotional pain emanates from confusing the things which are up to us and those that aren't. Fighting with reality, fighting with the things we cannot change, will leave us disturbed, angry at the world, blaming others, resenting life, and hating the gods.

Whenever we desire something that isn't in our power, our tranquility and confidence will be disturbed; if we don't get what we want, we'll be upset, and if we do get what we want, we'll experience anxiety and insecurity in the process of getting it as we can never be sure we'll get it. Therefore, we should always focus on what is up to us; that way we won't blame others, won't resent life, and surely won't fight with the gods. That's where much of the power of Stoicism comes from. The internalization of this basic truth that we can control our actions but not their outcomes makes us confident because we have given all that was in our power, and this confidence lets us calmly accept whatever happens.

Focus on what you control, and take the rest as it happens. The *rest* is not under your control, that's why the Stoics advise to accept it even if it's not pleasing. Accept it first, and then try to make the best out of it. We should accept rather than fight every little thing. If this guy cuts you off, then so be it. If your grades are bad, then they are, you've had your chance to prepare better. If the train is late, then it is late. Maybe it's good that it's late. Who knows? All you know is that the train isn't here yet. And that's okay, because it's someone else who drives the train.

The Stoics want us to cultivate acceptance to whatever happens because most events happen without us having a say in the matter. You can either take it as it comes and try to enjoy, or you can be reluctant and get dragged along anyway. There's a wonderful metaphor the Stoics use to explain this. Imagine a dog leashed to a moving cart. The leash is long enough to give the dog two options: (1) either he can smoothly follow the direction of the cart, over which he has no control, and at the same time enjoy the ride and explore the surroundings, (2) or he can stubbornly resist the cart with all his force and end up being dragged alongside anyway— for the rest of the ride.

Just like for that dog, there are many things in our lives we can't control. Either we accept the situation and try to make the best with it, or we fight it like a stubborn baby and end up crying and feeling miserable. It's our choice. In Ryan Holiday's words: "To get upset by things is to wrongly assume that they will last, [and] to resent change is to wrongly assume that you have a choice in the matter." That's why we should take Epictetus' advice to heart: "Seek not for events to happen as you wish but rather wish for events to happen as they do and your life will go smoothly." Very simple (yet not easy—we'll look at different exercises in Part 2).

Things happen that seem very unfortunate, no question. Loved ones die, a flood destroys your home, you lose your job, or fail your exams. You can't undo those conditions, you can only try to bear them with a noble spirit, and try to make the best with the given situation. Stoic philosophy teaches to focus on what you control, take the rest as it happens, and try to make the best out of it. It's what you do with a given situation that matters, and the way you go about doing it. The outcome, on the other hand, is beyond your control and doesn't matter much.

That's the kind of person Epictetus is looking for, "Find me a single man who cares how he does what he does, and is interested, not in what he can get, but in the manner of his own actions."

Attention: Taking the rest as it happens has nothing to do with resignation. Just because the Stoics said that many things are not within our power and that we should take any outcomes with equanimity does not mean that they were unambitious, feeling helpless, or into resignation. On the contrary, resignation is precisely *against* what the Stoics preached and practiced. Events do not happen as they do *regardless* of your actions, but rather *depending* on your actions. With your voluntary actions, you can co-direct the outcomes. It matters greatly how hard you train and try to hit the target, it's just not entirely up to you whether you hit or miss.

The argument that you could just resign if you should love whatever happens is ignorant and just plain lazy. It takes much more to accept rather than fight everything that happens. It takes a real man or woman to face necessity, and it takes a tough yet humble mind to accept and deal with misfortune. In other words, it takes a warrior-philosopher. Because a warrior takes everything as a challenge to become their best, while an ordinary person just takes everything either as a blessing or curse.

Just because we should try to accept whatever happens does not mean we approve of it. It just means that we understand that we cannot change it. And thus the best option is to accept it—and out of this acceptance, try to make the best out of it. "No one wants their children to get sick, no one wants to be in a car accident; but when these things happen, how can it be helpful to mentally argue with them?" That's how Byron Katie puts it in her book *Loving What Is*. Sure, things suck sometimes, but it doesn't help to fight them, neither does it help to give up and feel helpless. What the Stoics say helps is to look at them as a *challenge*, as a blank block of marble where we can train to express our best and ultimately become stronger.

The Stoics did not resign—they were committed to take appropriate action in the world. Marcus Aurelius was the most powerful military and political leader of his lifetime and led his armies into countless battles to protect the Roman Empire. He was *wise* enough to know the difference between what's up to him and what's not, *courageous* enough to focus and act upon his powers, and *calm* enough to take what's out of hand with equanimity so it wouldn't affect his wellbeing (see the Serenity Prayer on page 59).

The Good, the Bad, and the Indifferent Things

"Of things some are good, some are bad, and some are indifferent." Epictetus and the Stoics did not only differentiate between what's up to us and what's not, but also between what is good, bad, and indifferent. Crucially, only the things which are up to us can be either good or bad, and all those that aren't up to us get classified as *indifferent*. This is why the Stoic archer takes any outcome with equanimity, because it's not up to them and is therefore ultimately indifferent. However, the Stoics used a finer distinction that defined hitting the target (or the apple) as a *preferred* indifferent. If the outcome was *completely* indifferent, then why would you try to hit the target in the first place? Before we look closer at that distinction, let's look at what good, bad, and indifferent things include:

- **Good things:** All that is virtue; wisdom, justice, courage, self-discipline.
- **Bad things:** All that is vice; folly, injustice, cowardice, intemperance.
- **Indifferent things:** Everything else; life & death, health & sickness, wealth & poverty, pleasure & pain, reputation & bad repute.

The good and bad things can only be found in your behavior. Expressing your highest self, as seen earlier, is sufficient for the happy and smoothly flowing life. Because it's all that is within our power. Our actions matter greatly, and the development of one's character is all that counts for the good life. Nothing external is needed. The same is true for an unhappy life—it comes from vicious behavior, no matter the external circumstances. The only *good*, then, is living in accordance with nature, fulfilling our natural potential, and thus living by the virtues of wisdom, justice, courage, and self-discipline. The *outcome* of our virtuous behavior, however, is down to fate, it's beyond our direct control, and therefore is neither good nor bad, but *indifferent*. If the things that aren't under our control could be good or bad, then we'd be destined to suffer because of our inability to do something about them. All good must necessarily come from ourselves.

The indifferent things often get summarized as *health, wealth, and reputation*; but basically, everything external, everything that is *not* up to us, gets classified as indifferent. By *indifferent,* the Stoics mean that these events are neutral and can neither help nor harm our flourishing as human beings, they're unimportant for the happy and smoothly flowing life. If we need those external things for the good life, that would be demoralizing for those lacking them. Therefore, we should learn to be indifferent toward indifferent things, and as discussed before, accept the rest as it happens instead of fighting with it. Remember, the Stoic archer is ready to take any outcome with equanimity, because it's beyond their control.

The term *indifference*, however, is slightly misleading since it indicates that these things have no value at all. That's not the case. Although these external things are irrelevant for the good life, some are *preferred* to others nonetheless. It makes intuitive sense to choose to be healthy rather than sick, rich rather than poor, and beautiful rather than ugly. Also, it's clear that William Tell preferred to hit the apple rather than his son. These are called *preferred* indifferents. If we could choose, we'd always take the better options. And that's the same for the Stoics, they seek those better options but do so in a detached manner. They'd rather have it but it's okay if they don't. And the highest priority remains living with areté, so they only seek those preferred indifferents as long as it doesn't interfere with expressing their highest version.

Friendship is the most important preferred indifferent for the Stoics. Our human nature is not only rational but also social and, therefore, we're naturally attracted to other people. And a good person always shows love, kindness, justice, and concern for his fellow human beings—for his brothers, neighbors, and strangers alike. Having wise and good friends is the most precious external thing in the world.

As Seneca writes, the wise man "desires friends, neighbors, and associates, no matter how much he is sufficient unto himself." We're able to live a happy life without friends, but we prefer *not* to.

Unlike in Hollywood movies, however, the Stoics would never value love higher than moral integrity. Whenever virtue is involved, all else needs to give way. "Love conquers all" might be romantic and make good films, but it's precisely the opposite of the Stoic priorities—not even love should be traded if the price is the compromising of your character. So go ahead and seek friendship, as long as it doesn't need you to break with virtue. It's better to endure loneliness, sickness, and poverty in an honorable manner than to seek friendship, health, and wealth in a shameful one. The good person will always pursue virtue and avoid vice at all costs.

It's simply fabulous how Seneca explained it: "Good people will do what they find honorable to do, even if it requires hard work; they'll do it even if it causes them injury; they'll do it even if it will bring danger. Again, they won't do what they find base, even if it brings wealth, pleasure, or power. Nothing will deter them from what is honorable, and nothing will lure them into what is base."

In Poker as in Life, You Can Win with Any Hand

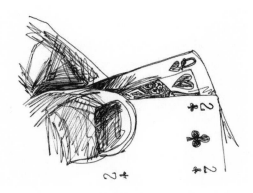

Poker explains this idea of good, bad, and indifferent things beautifully. The hands you're dealt are different external circumstances and life situations: your flat screen TV, your mean boss, the illness of your wife, the bad grades of your son, and your encouraging best friend. These are the various hands you're dealt and now have to play with. The hands are dealt by chance; you have no say in what you get. So the cards don't matter, they're neutral, indifferent. What matters is how well you play them.

In poker as in life, you can win with any hand. Sure, you prefer double ace and a healthy wife, but that's not up to you. What's up to you is what you *do* with the given situation. Once the hand has been dealt, you have no choice but accept what's too late to change, and you wish no longer for a more preferable hand but for the strength to play it the best you can.

The hallmark of an admirable player, then, is that they play their best regardless of their cards and that they calmly accept whatever comes out. It's all they can do—giving their best with whichever cards they've been dealt. In the end, not the player with the best cards, but the player who plays their cards the best over the course of the tournament, or the course of a whole lifetime, will win.

The best hand—great health, wealth, and fame—by itself cannot help a foolish and unjust person to attain the good life. And neither can the worst hand—sickness, poverty, and bad reputation—harm the virtuous person's wellbeing. On a scale, virtue and a good character will always outweigh health, wealth, and reputation. No abundance of external goods will ever keep up with a person's character. Some external goods might be preferable over others, but they're ultimately indifferent; all that matters for the good life is how we play them.

To a good person, losing his whole estate is the same as losing one penny, and being sick is no worse than having stumbled, that's what early Stoic Chrysippus supposedly said. Seneca eloquently expressed something similar, "Life is neither good nor bad; it is the space for both good and bad." Life and all its various situations can be used wisely or foolishly, it's our actions that make them good or bad. That's important. Although external things are indifferent, how we handle them is not. It's exactly the way of use of indifferent things that makes a happy or crappy life.

3. Take Responsibility: Get Good from Yourself

"If you want anything good, you must get it from yourself."

– EPICTETUS

The final corner of the Stoic Happiness Triangle is built upon the two others; they make this third corner possible. The first principle makes living with areté, or expressing your highest self, the highest good, whereas the second tells us that external circumstances are not important for the good life because they're not under our control. That means areté *alone* is enough for the good life, and because it's within our control, it makes us *responsible* for our own flourishing.

This is "the toughest and most appealing aspect of Stoicism," as Donald Robertson puts it, because this responsibility deprives us of any excuses for not attaining the happy and smoothly flowing life we all aspire to. We're the only ones stopping us from cultivating virtuous behavior, we're the only ones stopping us from living the good life.

Living with areté is within our control
+ things outside our control are not relevant for the happy life
= living with areté is within our control & enough for the happy life.
This results in us being responsible for our own happy lives.

Let's unravel this a bit more. The ultimate goal is eudaimonia—a happy and smoothly flowing life. In order to reach that goal, the Stoics defined another goal: *Living with areté* or *living in accordance with nature.* The human nature is to apply reason to our intentions and actions. So the goal to live with areté is to apply reason to our actions and always try to express our highest version of ourselves.

In modern terms, this is a *process* goal. The Stoics did not focus on the *future* outcome (a happy life) but on the process in the *present moment* (living with areté) that should ultimately lead to the wished outcome. This focus on the process is what makes us, as aspiring Stoics, ultimately responsible for our own flourishing because we're in control of that process. While the outcome can be prevented by external events, the process and our intentions are completed in the present moment and cannot be prevented by anything outside our control.

As Seneca puts it, "The wise man looks to the purpose of all actions, not their consequences; beginnings are in our power but Fortune judges the outcome, and I do not grant her a verdict upon me."

Stoicism teaches that we're very much responsible for our own happiness as well as unhappiness. It also teaches that taking this responsibility will improve our chances of attaining eudaimonia. The *victim mentality*—blaming external circumstances for our unhappiness—on the other hand, will make the happy life an impossible goal to reach.

We must refuse to let the hands we're dealt decide over our wellbeing. The Stoics say that outside events and other people may have the power to affect how and even whether you live, but they don't have the power to ruin our lives. Only you yourself can ruin your life by getting jerked around by things you don't control and by failing to act as well as you're capable of.

We must make sure that our happiness depends as little as possible on outside circumstances. There should be only a loose connection between what happens to us and how happy we are. That's possible by focusing on what we control and trying to make the best with the given circumstances. And also by wanting only what is within our power, because as learned earlier, desiring what's *not* within our power is the root cause of emotional suffering.

"It is never possible to make happiness consistent with a longing after what is not present. For true happiness implies the possession of all which is desired, as in case of satiety with food; there must be no thirst, no hunger." What Epictetus describes here is exactly what we today call *conditional happiness*—binding happiness to some future event. I'll be happy *after* my exams. I'll be happy *when* I get that new Porsche 911. I'll be happy *when* I finally earn six figures. It's like the horizon—you can walk for miles and miles but won't get any closer. Either we keep on yearning for stuff we don't have, or we actually have a chance for happiness. We can't have both. True happiness is when you have *all* you desire.

"Externals are not in my power; will is in my power. Where shall I seek the good and the bad? Within, in the things which are my own. But in what does not belong to you call nothing either good or bad." Epictetus reminds us here to seek the good within ourselves. He often uses the basic message, "If you want anything good, get it from yourself." We must seek happiness within ourselves, not in external things; they're not within our power, they're neither good nor bad but indifferent.

Nature equipped us with the necessary tools to create a satisfactory and happy life no matter the hardships we face in life. So, if we want to gain contentment, we must change ourselves and our desires. We cannot change the things that happen in the world around us, we can only change the way we look at those things and what we *choose* to make out of them.

Changing outside events is impossible.

Changing your view about those events is possible.

So why not try to change what's possible?

The Freedom of Choice

"There are three things in your composition: body, breath, and mind," Marcus Aurelius reminds himself. "The first two are yours to the extent that you must take care for them, but only the third is in the full sense your own." Only the mind is truly yours. Only the mind is within the Stoic circle of control. All else is not or only partially within our control.

As discussed earlier, our actions are within our power, but not their outcomes. Fortunately, Epictetus says, "the most excellent and superior faculty"—our ability to use reason—was also placed within our power, so that we can make "the right use of the appearances of things." Even if we're "only" given control over our mind, this leaves us with plenty of power—the ability to decide what outside events will mean to us. *Judgment*, then, becomes the heart of our being of rational creatures, and the source of our freedom.

We don't control what happens in the world around us, but we do have the power to control our opinions about these events. "We cannot choose our external circumstances, but we can always choose how we respond to them," as Epictetus tells us. We must realize that external events are neutral, and only how we choose to react to them makes them good or bad.

Either we're a victim to our circumstances and get jerked around like our voodoo doll, or we choose to stand responsible for how we handle the circumstances, and make sure we don't let ourselves jerk around. Being a helpless victim is never helpful. Taking responsibility, on the other hand, gives us the power to make the best with the given circumstances.

Every outside event, then, offers an area of our own control, namely what we make with that event. This is a true and fair amount of control, stemming from our ability to judge events as we choose to. Being able to *choose* means we have a choice, and having a choice means freedom. Let's call this the *freedom of choice*, inspired by Viktor Frankl, who says in his book *A Man's Search for Meaning,* "Everything can be taken from a man but one thing; the last of the human freedoms—to choose one's attitude in any given set of circumstances."

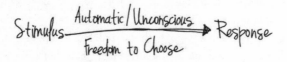

Stimulus ——— Automatic / Unconscious / Freedom to Choose ——▶ Response

Something happens (stimulus) and then we react to it (response). Oftentimes, this response happens automatically, unconsciously, and without us thinking about it. We can easily observe this behavior in other people—something happens and they react impulsively. In kids, that's even more distinct. Let's say young Boy is playing with his brontosaur Bronty, and then you take it away. What happens? Chances are high that Boy will immediately start crying. Boy doesn't think about his reaction, it will come automatically. Maybe he'll stare at you in disbelief before he'll start *laughing*. Who knows? Now, Boy and other young kids don't have the power to choose a response. But for you and me, it's different. Potentially, there's a small gap between stimulus and response. The power lies in that gap. The freedom of choice lies in that gap.

The gap means that we have the chance to step in between stimulus and response and choose our voluntary reaction (or *non*-reaction). The gap is only a *potential* gap because if we're not aware enough, there will be no gap, and we will mindlessly go with the default (or auto-) response. Awareness, mindfulness, or *attention* as the Stoics call it, is necessary for you to be able to step in between stimulus and response. Depending on your awareness, the gap becomes bigger or smaller or even nonexistent.

The point is, when something happens to you—you break a glass, step into dog poop, or get shown the middle finger by a stranger—you could enter the gap before you react automatically. Once you're in the gap, you can think about your options, and then *choose* your best reaction. Most people will reactively go with their default response, and only later (or not at all) realize that their reaction was inappropriate.

When you step into dog poop, it's plausible that some reaction follows automatically. Something inside you decides that the situation is really bad; what follows are feelings of anger, annoyance, and panic, accompanied by swear words and hectic body movements. Now this might not seem too bad, but what happens is that you get jerked around by an outside event that you can't change anymore. You let an outside circumstance determine how you feel. If we generally go with our default reactions, we'll always be dependent on what happens around us; stepping into dog poop makes us miserable, stepping on a $10 bill makes us happy. We're at the mercy of the situation, if our default reaction to the situation is positive, then *hurray*, if not, then *waah*. That is throwing our voodoo doll out in the streets all over again. Fortunately, it doesn't need to be that way.

The Stoics argue that you can step in between what happens (dog poop), and your reaction to it (anger and f-words). The idea is to choose your best virtuous response rather than going with the default. In order to do that, you need to be able to *spot* your automatic impression (it's really bad) in the first place. If you want to get in the gap and choose your response, you need the awareness to spot the first impression that arises in the form of thoughts and/or emotions. Once you see this first impression, you can step back, and question whether this impression is good to go with or not. You can look at this thought impression as a mere hypothesis up for debate before you examine it rationally.

Basically, you *withhold* the approval of that impression and avoid rash, impulsive, and automatic behavior. This is immensely powerful and enables you to think before you (re-)act. It gives you the power to choose the best possible reaction, and what happens in the world around you doesn't matter so much anymore. It hands you the key to your ideal behavior as you can choose to act in a wise, serene, and forgiving way—smile, clean the shoe, and move on with your life.

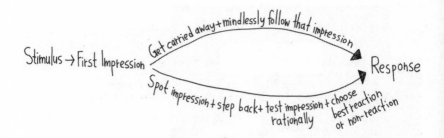

The freedom of choice, or how the Stoics call it, *reasoned choice*, is really about actively choosing our response rather than reactively going with the default response. In order to be able to do that, we need to bring awareness into the situation so we can spot our first impression and avoid getting carried away by it and respond reactively. The reactive response could be unvirtuous behavior and cause further unhealthy emotions such as anger, fear, or desire. Instead, if we're able to step back from the initial impression, we can evaluate that impression rationally, look at other possible responses, and then choose our best reaction or non-reaction (sometimes it's best to not react at all). That way we respond how we choose to, hopefully in accordance with virtue.

The Mind Makes You Rich, Even in Exile

How did the Stoics react to adversity? Three of our four protagonists had been exiled at least once. They took it in exemplary Stoic manner. Seneca said, "It is the mind that makes us rich; this goes with us into exile." Musonius Rufus, who was exiled to the worst of all places, Gyaros, said that exile deprived him of his country but not of his ability to endure exile. He even said that exile doesn't deprive a person of anything of value—virtue cannot be taken away. Exile doesn't prevent you from being courageous and just. We must keep in mind that happiness depends more on what we make of what happens rather than what happens in the first place. No matter what happens to you, your mind is always available to turn it into good fortune by responding with virtue.

The Stoic Sage, and apparently also the main philosophers, are absolutely free even in exile. Because their freedom consists in being able to follow their reasonable nature, which is to focus on what you control, take the rest as it happens, and respond with virtue. Every obstacle becomes an opportunity to practice wisdom, courage, justice, and self-discipline. The ideal Stoic only wants to respond to whatever happens in harmony with reason and his highest self, and nothing can prevent him from doing that. He only desires what's within his control, and therefore he remains "free" even in exile or prison.

Stoicism challenges you to change yourself whenever you can't change the situation. Even if you can't change the situation, you have the power to change your attitude about it and respond with virtue. No matter where you are (prison or palace), and no matter what challenge you're facing (dog poop or $10 bill), your freedom of choice will always be available to you; you just need to spot your first impression, avoid pooping a brick, take a step back instead, evaluate the situation, and choose your wisest response. External events are not what matters, but what you choose to do with them.

We must recognize the fact that we're *response*-able to choose how to *respond* to situations. Viktor Frankl, the legend who came up with the *freedom of choice*, went through the most brutal experiences we can imagine. He lost his whole family and barely survived the horrors of the Nazi concentration camps of World War II. Despite those horrors, he was still able to choose his attitude and he chose to not give in to those terrible situations. Sure, we've all experienced many bad things in our lives, but most certainly not as barbarous as losing our entire family and going through concentration camps. The point is, if Frankl was able to choose his response in the midst of unspeakable terror, then we should be able to choose our responses too. (Speaking of Viktor Frankl, if you haven't already, make sure to read his book *A Man's Search for Meaning*.)

Attention: Although Stoic philosophers say we can step in between stimulus and response, they admit that there are automatic reactions we don't control. These are reflex-like emotional reactions to some impressions such as blushing, sweating, tension, tears, or startling. We have no choice but accept these rapid bodily reactions. A sudden noise can shock you without you having a say in it. However, if we bring enough awareness into the situation, we can spot our impression, step back, and avoid getting carried away by it. Even if you don't control these immediate reflexive reactions, you have the power to control what comes next: go along with the impression or step back, evaluate the situation, and choose a response consistent with your values.

Disturbed or Invincible: That's Up to You

"Men are disturbed not by the things which happen, but by the opinions about the things." Epictetus' words are an important take-away from what we've just learned: External events are not within our power but they offer an area we control; we have the power to choose what these events mean to us, and it's our choices that matter, not the events. External events basically carry no meaning at all, it's how we perceive them, it's our judgments that give them meaning and make them seem good or bad.

(By the way, this is far from easy to realize as long as people respond impulsively and therefore mindlessly to events, because it seems obvious to them that the event causes their unhappiness. As soon as they get better at stepping back from their initial impressions, they'll see that what upsets them is their very own judgment about the situation.)

The first lesson, then, is to never blame other people or outside events for whatever negative emotions we're feeling. Take responsibility. For the Stoics, it's clear that not events, but our opinions about those events are the cause of a troubled mind. This might show as suffering and unhappiness and arises when we believe the stories we tell ourselves. An impression comes as a thought into our heads and we accept it as the truth. "I'm in exile, this is terrible." The situation itself (exile) does *not* make us unhappy, it may cause physical pain in certain situations, but it's the story about the situation (it's terrible) that causes the trouble. Your judgments in form of thoughts, opinions, and interpretations make you unhappy. Good or bad can only be found in your judgments and actions, not in external events.

The troubled mind comes from judging an event as undesirable or bad, often in the form of complaining. We give an event value by judging it as *terrible* for example, and forget that the event itself is neither good nor bad; it is empty and carries no meaning at all. We give it the meaning by judging, resenting, and wanting it to be different. This causes the emotional suffering. If you could let it be as it is, if you were able *not* to judge it good or bad but take it *as it is* (neutral, indifferent), then you wouldn't have a troubled mind. You are free of suffering, says Epictetus, if you don't care for the things which are not in your power.

- *Duh, I'm so clumsy.* **Vs.** *The glass is broken.*
- *This is the worst day of my life!* **Vs.** *There's dog poop on my shoe sole. It smells.*
- *Argh, such a jerk! I hate this guy.* **Vs.** *He erected the middle finger in my direction.*

The events themselves carry no meaning. It's our judgments that make them either good or bad. I like how Ellie Goulding sings in her song *First Time*, "The middle finger was our peace sign." When you think about it this way, "Argh, such a jerk!" can easily become a smile and, "Aww, such a sweetie." The exact same event can be interpreted in so many different ways and arouse complete opposite feelings.

Look, I know you're not stupid and know very well what the other person is trying to tell you; the point is, it doesn't matter what he's trying to tell you, what matters is what you make out of it. So even if it seems (or it's obvious) that someone is trying to insult you, it's *your judgment* that provokes you. You cannot be harmed unless you let it, because the other person has no access to your mind. "Otherwise," Marcus Aurelius says, "my neighbor's wickedness would be my own harm: and this was not in god's intention, to leave my misfortune up to another." Only you yourself have access to your mind, and only you can ruin your life. You're responsible.

Someone can't frustrate *you*, dog poop can't make *you* depressed—these are external events that have no access to your mind. Those emotions you feel, as real as they are, don't come from the outside, but from the inside. *You* generate those emotions, *you* generate your pain. A broken glass is a broken glass. It's your judgment ("Duh, I'm so clumsy") that makes you feel like a loser. Don't blame the event, blame your reactive self for feeling how you feel. The cause lies in your judgment. "Remove the judgment," Marcus says, "and the hurt itself is removed." Don't judge the event, and you won't get harmed. Your *reaction,* then, basically shows whether you've been harmed or not. When you break a glass, you have two options: Get hurt, or don't get hurt.

"Duh, I'm so clumsy" + start crying and feel miserable = strong reaction, getting hurt.

"Oops" + clean up and move on with your life = no reaction, not getting hurt.

This gives you plenty of power, because it means you cannot get upset by anything outside your control. Only your judgment can harm you. No matter what uncontrollable challenges you're facing in life, you have the power to decide what these events mean to you, only you have the freedom to choose your best reaction. Your reaction will either delight or harm you.

That's why Epictetus advises to always have two rules ready at mind: (1) there is nothing good or bad unless we choose to make it so, and (2) we shouldn't try to lead events but follow them. Resistance is futile, take things as they come, and make the best of what's in your power.

Chapter 4

The Villain: Negative Emotions Get in the Way

"Once [anger] begins to carry us away, it is hard to get back
again into a healthy condition, because reason goes for
nothing once passion has been admitted to the mind . . .
The enemy must be met and driven back at the outermost
frontier-line: for when he has once entered the city and
passed its gates, he will not allow his prisoners to set
bounds to his victory."

– SENECA

Happiness seems pretty doable, right? For the Stoics, it only
consists in how we respond to events, and what we make of
them. Aligning our actions with virtue is sufficient (but also
necessary) for the happy and smoothly flowing life. So what
happens? Why don't we all get there with a snap of the
fingers?

Life gets in the way. Reality erects itself in front of us; it
catches us by surprise, seems overwhelming, causes fear,
insecurity, anger, and grief, and makes us want to run away

87

and hide. Things are tougher than we thought, and they happen differently than we expected and wished for, and we're struggling to deal with them effectively, or even to accept them in the first place. But wait! Stoicism teaches that external events do *not* matter and that we must get any good from ourselves. It only *seems* that life gets in the way; in reality, it's our negative emotions that get in the way. These intense emotions conquer our mind, actually our whole being, make it impossible to think clearly, and urge us to do the opposite of what we think is right.

Once our mind has been captured by negative emotions, or *passions* as the Stoics call them, such as irrational fear, grief, anger, or greed, these passions take over, and we react impulsively without being able to think about it. As Seneca says in the opening lines to this chapter, once the enemy has entered the mind, reason is gone. It's one or the other, reason or passion; when passion is at the steering wheel, reason is tied up and gagged in the trunk.

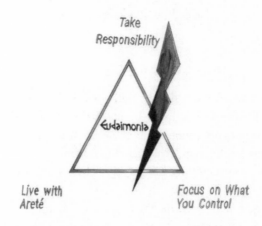

Take
Responsibility

Eudaimonia

Live with
Areté

Focus on What
You Control

Negative emotions naturally feel *bad*; think of grief, fear, jealousy, or strong cravings. So with the emotion in the driver's seat, and with something inside feeling bad, our number one priority (unconsciously) becomes to feel *better*, and we automatically seek relief of the pain we're feeling. The negative emotion orders us to do what makes us feel better and relieve the pain in the present moment, regardless of our values and long-term goals. We end up pushing aside our deep values, and instead walk away like a coward, order pizza and tiramisu, binge-watch Marvel movies, smash doors and glasses, shout at our friends and kids, and buy those black high heels we don't need.

Negative emotions can take countless forms. They can swallow us completely like intense anger which creates a sudden tunnel vision that simply lets us act out—bam!—and it's happened. They can be much calmer like excessive grief which can leave us full of self-pity, depressive thoughts, and complete inaction. Or they can be very subtle like "just not feeling like it," which can stem from different emotions and causes us simply to *not* do what we know we *should* be doing (ever heard of procrastination?).

For example, when I was a teenager, a friend of mine got beaten up by another guy from school. Other kids and I were watching, and I knew it would be right to help, but something inside was holding me back; I didn't feel like helping, I was afraid. The emotion won. Or all the times I saw some beautiful girl in a bar and wanted to say hello, but at the same time I didn't feel like it. I was afraid. The emotion won most times. Of course I had some great excuses; she wasn't *that* pretty, I just wasn't in the mood, I was there for the good time with the lads, and so on.

It doesn't really matter which emotions get in the way—for me it's obviously fear in many cases (I'm working on it), for you it might be anger, greed, resentment, or pride. The problem with these emotions is not that they exist, but that they overwhelm us so that we end up doing the opposite of what we ought to do. And as we learned earlier, our rational actions are at the root of our happiness, therefore we can't live a happy life when we let strong emotional disturbances dictate our actions. The Stoics believed that such passions are toxic to the good life and cause misery for many people. The majority of us are enslaved by these emotions; we too often act according to our emotions instead of our values.

So the Stoics want us to overcome these irrational fears and desires, so that we're able to act according to virtue and attain true happiness. Also, oftentimes, these emotions are against our rational nature as they ignore what is truly good. When I'm afraid to say hello to some girl, this fear and my inaction goes completely against virtue—it's unwise and irrational to fear what's not dangerous, it lacks self-discipline for not overcoming the inner resistance, and it's simply cowardly. It's essential to overcome these negative emotions if we want to practice Stoicism. This is why a key part of the Stoic philosophy is to prevent the onset of negative emotions, and to be prepared to deal with them effectively and not get overwhelmed if they arise nevertheless (and they will!)

So what's the secret? There's not really a secret (sorry!). However, there are specific practices that'll help you prepare for challenging situations. (These practices are covered in the second part of this book.) After a quick side note, we'll look at the two main reasons why negative emotions conquer us in the first place. When we can minimize these two, then we'll consequently get less negative emotions, and we'll get better at dealing with them.

Attention: Our human brain is built for survival, not thriving. Our ancestors' main goals were to survive and replicate. Food and water were scarce. And there were many dangers, so they were constantly on the lookout for dangerous animals and rival clans. That's why our brains developed a *negativity bias*—if they got caught by surprise by a wolf, they were dead. On the other hand, if they missed an opportunity for food, they still had another chance. So it was more important to focus on the negative rather than the positive.

And today, we still have these same brains—constantly checking if what's happening around us is dangerous. Because of our evolution, we see obstacles much better than opportunities. It's in our nature to worry about health, wealth, and social status. It seems we need those for survival. Therefore, we automatically compare ourselves to others, focus on possible dangers, and chase more and more stuff.

So don't worry if you think you're always negative, that's normal. That's just the built-in negativity bias of our brain. However, that's highly counterproductive in the modern world as, after all, we're very safe and have enough food— therefore, survival can be ticked off for the most part. Nothing is going to attack you at night, and no rival clan will burn down your hut. The point is, these negative emotions get in the way and we must try to minimize them and the effects they have on our lives. Let's now look at the two main reasons why we get overwhelmed by negative emotions.

We Want What's Beyond Our Control

"Passion is produced no otherwise than by a disappointment of one's desires." Epictetus makes the point that negative emotions arise when we don't get what we want. This disappointment "is the spring of sorrow, lamentation, and envy; this renders us envious and emulous, and incapable of hearing reason."

Basically, negative emotions come from wanting and fearing what's not under our control. As we learned earlier, the root cause of our suffering stems from worrying about stuff outside our control. These are faulty value judgments; we value some *indifferent* external thing as good or bad. For example, mistakenly judging material things as *good* or desirable is the cause of cravings for wealth and pleasure. Such strong craving is a negative emotion that takes over the steering wheel and lets us do whatever satisfies the craving for the moment, regardless of our values. Because we're incapable to hear reason, remember, reason is tied up and gagged in the trunk.

Faulty value judgments also work the other way around. We mistakenly judge some indifferent external event such as rain, annoying people, or poverty as *bad* or even terrible, and this wrong judgment about the event causes anger or fear. So it's the wrong judgment about an event that causes the negative emotions, and these emotions, again, get in the way of a happy life because they let us act impulsively rather than rationally.

Donald Robertson says it well in his book *Stoicism and the Art of Happiness,* "The majority of ordinary people lack fulfillment and peace of mind because their values are confused and internally conflicted. We waste our lives chasing after an illusion of Happiness, based on a mixture of hedonism, materialism and egotism—crazy, self-defeating values absorbed from the foolish world around us."

We desire and fear external things beyond our direct control; we naively judge indifferent things such as health, wealth, and reputation as good and even necessary for the happy life, and we also judge sickness, poverty, and ridicule as bad and hindering to the happy life. These desires and fears about external things are a bright blinking warning sign that says, "You forgot the basics! Go back and engrain the core beliefs." In other words, we haven't yet second natur*ed* the basic Stoic principles that virtue is the only true good, that what's not within our control is ultimately indifferent, and that we are solely responsible for our flourishing. As long as we feel that things happen for or against us, that dog poop makes a miserable day, and a bonus makes a happy one, as long as we're afraid of not getting what we want and feel bad about not getting it—we're only a puppet to our emotions, caused by faulty judgments about what's truly good and bad.

"You are silly," Epictetus says, "[if] you would have the things which are not in your power to be in your power, and the things which belong to others to be yours." If we could carefully separate between the things which are up to us and the things which are not, and focus on those up to us and let the rest happen as it will, then we'd get much less jerked around by the negative emotions caused by faulty judgments.

However, even if we set out to do exactly that, there's something else that often gets in the way: unconsciousness. We're not aware enough in situations and forget to focus on what we can control; instead, we get carried away by our initial impressions and will only realize later that we misjudged the event. A lack of awareness is the second reason for negative emotions to arise and take us over.

We Lack Awareness and Get Carried Away by Impressions

Do you remember that the Stoics want us to pay massive attention to our every action? Just like when we're paying attention not to stand on bits of broken glass? Well, guess what happens when we don't bring such attention into challenging situations? We get carried away by our first impressions without being able to check them. These first impressions are like *tendencies* to act a certain way, but when we're aware enough, we can step in and choose our best response, which is most certainly different to the first impression.

Here's an example that happened to me when I took a toilet break. I got up from my writing chair, walked to the toilet, when the new pack of toilet paper on the flushing tank caught my attention. I bought it yesterday when I did my grocery shopping, and it was necessary to do so. After seeing it, my mind immediately went, "Yeah, you did very well buying it. Nils (my brother I live with) didn't even notice. No signs of gratitude, and so on." Feelings of light anger and unease started to arise within, and my mind went on rationalizing itself, "Well, he did say *thank you* for buying the groceries. And he does many other things in the household, and so on." Fortunately I was aware enough to recognize this thought pattern, stepped in, and called it off as classic *ego-wants-recognition* mind battle. The negative feelings were gone in the blink of an eye.

What happened exactly? The situation *new toilet paper* caused an automatic first impression of *such and such is bad* with a tendency toward getting angry. Thankfully, I was aware enough, recognized it, and could call it off immediately. If it would have been a more challenging situation, then I'd have been able to use reason, or just cold hard logic, and look at the situation objectively. I'd have said to myself that doing the right thing is enough, it's a reward in itself, and doesn't need recognition from someone else. Now, if I'd been unaware of that irrational impression, I'd have gotten angry and frustrated and entered my brother's room and kicked him in the face. Or, more likely, the negative impression would have carried me away and I would have been lost in thought for a time while being irrationally angry with my brother.

That's why unawareness is so dangerous: While being unaware, we can't observe and recognize our first impressions and would mindlessly follow along. As Epictetus says, "When you have let your mind loose, it is no longer in your power to recall it, either to propriety, or to modesty, or to moderation: but you do everything that comes into your mind in obedience to your inclinations." That's exactly what we learned earlier—once passion has taken over, we obey like a dog that smells sausage. Reason can shout and whistle her lungs out, but we can't hear her because we're completely absorbed by passion's sausage.

Look, one could argue that the reason for the negative emotions to take over even in this case is the faulty judgment, not the unawareness. The emotions arise because of the irrational judgment that my brother is ungrateful. However, one could also argue that many faulty judgments happen because we're not aware enough in the first place. We're not aware of our every step and end up in dog poop. Or my mom isn't aware enough to know how much of her cup of coffee she's already drank so she ends up wondering, "Who drank my coffee?" Sure, she might value coffee too highly (is that even possible?), but the reason behind that faulty judgment is her unawareness while drinking it herself—in most cases (sorry mom, sometimes I took a sip or two).

The point is, being aware will reduce the times we get taken over by negative emotions. This is important because getting taken over by negative emotions is exactly what hinders us from taking the right actions and getting the good life. Remember, for the Stoics, the only good lies in our voluntary actions, and our actions can only be voluntary when we're bringing awareness into every moment. If we lack that awareness, we permit ourselves to get carried away and let our actions become *shameful and disregardful*, to use Epictetus' words. Only by bringing awareness into the moment, we can properly confront the challenge of accepting external events with equanimity, while cultivating wisdom, justice, and self-discipline in our reactions. With that awareness, we can try to follow Epictetus' advice to *endure and renounce* in everyday situations:

1. We should *endure* what we irrationally fear and dislike with courage and perseverance.

2. We should *renounce* (or abstain from) what we irrationally crave through discretion and self-discipline.

We definitely need awareness to detect irrational fears and cravings before we can *endure* them with courage and perseverance, or *abstain from* them with discretion and self-discipline. Awareness, however, won't be enough. Not everybody can stare fear in the eyes and do it anyway. I often can't. Even if I'm aware enough to recognize my fear while knowing the fear is irrational and it would be the wise thing to act despite the fear, the emotion often beats my courage. Another example is the battle between an irrational desire and self-discipline. After a long day of work and persevering with my tasks, I observe the desire to check some news. I'm well aware of the battle between the pleasurable desire and my deflating willpower, and most times willpower wins, but sometimes I give in to the desire.

Awareness might not be enough to always act accordingly to our values, but it surely buys you time and delay, so you see the situation clearly and can at least try to make the rational decision. This will make it way easier to master yourself, act rationally, and make progress toward the happy and smoothly flowing life. And it will prevent you many times from getting carried away by irrational emotions, and you'll step into folly (and dog poop) less frequently.

Step by step, you get ahead.

PART 2

55 Stoic Practices

"Let philosophy scrape off your own faults,
rather than be a way to rail against the faults of others."
– SENECA

Chapter 5

How to Practice Stoicism?

"As it is we are glib and fluent in the lecture-room, and if any
paltry question arises about a point of conduct, we are
capable of pursuing the subject logically; but put us to the
practical test and you will find us miserable shipwrecks."

– EPICTETUS

Congratulations! You made it through the theory part. It's
time to get in the water.

Beware though, just because we're fluent in the
classroom doesn't mean we're ready for the real world.
Knowing the theory and applying it in practice are two
entirely different animals. You are going to get wet.

Or as Epictetus puts it, we might get miserably
shipwrecked. That's why we must practice. He says a
carpenter becomes a carpenter by learning certain things.
And a helmsman becomes a helmsman by learning certain
things. So it's clear that if we want to become good people,
we must learn certain things.

"Step forward," he says, "and make use of what you've
learned. It isn't more logic chopping that is needed—our
Stoic texts are full of that. What we need now are people to

apply their learning and bear witness to their learning in their actions. Please, be the one to take on this character, I am tired in my teaching of invoking examples from the past, I want to be able to hold up an example from my time."

Be the example out there. Don't be satisfied with mere learning, but practice, practice, practice! Because if time passes, Epictetus says, we forget what we've learned and end up doing the opposite, and hold opinions the opposite of what we should.

Sorry to bring it to you, but you're not Superman. You can't just hear Stoic principles once and expect to rely on them when life happens. You must practice like a professional athlete, and show up on the pitch every day. Show up earlier and leave later than everyone else. From nothing comes nothing.

Remember, philosophy is all about how to live one's life. As discussed earlier, Epictetus compares philosophy to artisans—just as the carpenter uses wood and the sculptor uses bronze, we use our own lives as the raw material in the art of living.

Every event in our lives presents a blank block of marble that we can train on. That's how we learn to use a chisel and mallet until we've mastered our craft. Philosophy is all about applying its principles to the real world. Remember, we want to be warrior-philosophers and put into practice what we learn.

That's what this part is all about. You'll find 55 Stoic practices mixed with practical advice. Each can be used by itself. For simplicity reasons, let's differentiate between three sorts of practices: The first are *preparing practices* you can do for yourself. You won't need a life situation to train on, and you can simply do them at home. The second are practices for *challenging life situations*: how to handle yourself in stressful moments. And the third are practices for *situations with other people*: how to deal with challenging people.

Keep in mind that different approaches work better for some people and worse for others. Treat the practices as suggestions, not as rigid rules. Try the practices and keep on doing what works and leave out what doesn't. Don't overthink it.

Now before we get to the practices, let's quickly look at a legend and three important details that will help you get the most out of the practices.

Brace Yourself

"What would have become of Hercules, do you think, if there had been no lion, hydra, stag or boar - and no savage criminals to rid the world of? What would he have done in the absence of such challenges?"

– EPICTETUS

What would have become of legendary Hercules without any struggles?

"Obviously," Epictetus says, "he would have just rolled over in bed and gone back to sleep. So by snoring his life away in luxury and comfort he never would have developed into the mighty Hercules."

What would have become of any person you admire without any struggles? Your mom? That colleague you rate so highly? Roger Federer or any other superstar?

One thing is sure, they wouldn't be where they are without the challenges they surely faced in their lives. Difficulties are important. That's what we're here for. God, says Seneca, "does not make a spoiled pet of a good man; he tests him, hardens him, and fits him for his own service."

All the adversities you're facing in your life, these are tests. It's mere training. Life isn't supposed to be easy, life is supposed to be challenging to make sure you actually grow. "And those things which we all shudder and tremble at are for the good of the persons themselves to whom they come," says Seneca.

Whenever you find yourself in a hole, remind yourself of Hercules who became strong only *because* of the challenges he faced.

Life is meant to be hard at times. Chin up, chest out, you'll do fine.

Now, let's look at three helpful details that'll help you get the most out of the practices.

Be Mindful

Stoicism isn't an easy-to-follow road. There are many principles to keep in mind and to live by.

And the most important prerequisite is to be aware of what's going on. Because Stoic philosophy is a lot about how we react to what happens in the world around us. What happens doesn't matter because it's beyond our control. What matters is how we deal with it.

In order to deal with what happens effectively and to be mindful of our reactions, we need to be aware of what's going on. We need to be able to step in between stimulus and response. We need to be able to *not* go with our impulses, but take a step back and look at the situation objectively.

Stoicism requires us to be able to not react impulsively to what happens to us. It requires us to spot our initial impressions, so that we recognize our ability to choose our response. Once we're able to spot our automatic impressions, we can test them and actively choose to go with the impression or not.

Look, awareness is the first step toward any serious change. If you're not aware of what's going wrong in your life, then how do you want to fix it? If you don't realize when you get angry, how do you want to prevent it in the future? "A consciousness of wrongdoing is the first step to salvation," Seneca says. "You have to catch yourself doing it before you can correct it."

Stoicism asks of us to be aware of what we do in every moment. The whole idea of virtue, to express our highest self in every moment, is based on our ability to be present in the moment and know what's going on. How else do we want to choose our best action?

Our voluntary thoughts and actions are by definition the only things within our control. And they only exist in the here and now. We can't choose an action if we're lost in thought, ruminating in the past, or dreaming about the future.

Therefore, we should focus our attention on the present moment, undistracted by the past or future. Then we can properly confront the challenge we're facing now, trying to accept it as it is, and choose a response consistent with our values.

Basically, we should be aware of our every step. As said earlier, we should watch ourselves like a hawk and bring the same attention into the moment as when we're walking barefoot on broken glass. This focused and continuous self-observation is needed to practice Stoicism effectively.

Don't worry if you think you're not a very mindful person. You're still able to practice most of the following practices. Plus, many will actually improve your mindfulness. This cultivation of awareness is a part of Stoicism. You'll get better at stepping back from your impulses, so you can analyze them and question their accuracy, and then decide upon your smartest response.

Recharge Your Self-Discipline

Practicing Stoicism isn't like watching TV. It takes effort. You must actually do something.

Most practices require self-discipline if you want to do them. Some are challenging, not particularly fun, and will suck up your willpower. But that's part of the game. And it's similar with other things in life. If you want to get better at darts, you must practice it. If you want to get better at lifting weights, you must train hard.

It's the same with Stoicism. It requires effort and discipline, but at the same time it will build up endurance and self-discipline. It will make you stronger. Just like lifting weights will make your muscles stronger, practicing Stoic principles will make your will stronger.

Yes, it's demanding. But you will always have to pay the price if you want to improve. The practices will make you more resilient, tranquil, courageous, disciplined, and so on.

Plus, you must keep in mind that there's a cost of *not* having and practicing a philosophy of life. Author William Irvine explains the cost bluntly: "The danger that you will spend your days pursuing valueless things and will therefore waste your life."

It's up to us. Either we're willing to invest and reap the benefits, or we're not and risk wasting our lives.

Look, the possible rewards are much greater than the effort you have to put into it. This investment is a no-brainer if you ask me. There's much to gain and nothing but a little effort to lose. Here's how Irvine describes what you'll get if you make the investment: "Stoics can transform themselves into individuals remarkable for their courage and self-control. They will be able to do things that others dread doing, and they will be able to refrain from doing things that others cannot resist doing."

You can become this remarkable individual if you're willing to put in some effort. Do those practices even if you don't feel like doing them. It's what you have to do. Don't read them, nod your head, and move on without putting in into practice. That won't make you any better.

Remember, self-discipline is like a muscle. The more you use it, the stronger it will get. So each time you decide to overcome the initial hurdle and do a practice, you train yourself in self-discipline and willpower.

If you do it today, you'll be more likely to do it tomorrow. If you don't do it today, you'll be less likely to do it tomorrow.

Don't Call Yourself a Philosopher

According to Epictetus, you'll get ridiculed for practicing Stoicism: "If you desire philosophy, prepare yourself from the beginning to be ridiculed, to expect that many will sneer at you."

Now, I don't know if that's still valid today. I don't talk much about practicing Stoicism so I haven't experienced people mocking me about it. Anyway, I think if friends do mock you for trying to improve yourself you might want to rethink those friendships.

"Remember," Epictetus continues, "that if you abide in the same principles, these men who first ridiculed will afterward admire you."

So even if you get ridiculed and others give you a hard time for your commitment to self-improvement, know that if you stay strong, these people will admire you.

The simplest trick to make sure nobody will mock you comes from Epictetus, too: "On no occasion call yourself a philosopher, and do not, for the most part, talk among laymen about your philosophical principles, but rather do what follows from your principles."

Don't mention that you're into Stoicism, just live by it. You can still tell those who want to know what's going on with you when they recognize your positive changes. That's the first tip William Irvine shares in his book *A Guide to the Good Life:* "The first tip I would offer to those wishing to give Stoicism a try is to practice what I have referred to as *stealth Stoicism*: You would do well, I think, to keep it a secret that you are a practicing Stoic. By practicing Stoicism stealthily, you can gain its benefits while avoiding one significant cost: the teasing and outright mockery of your friends, relatives, neighbors, and coworkers."

Demonstrate rather than instruct what you learn.

Dive in.

Chapter 6

Preparing Practices

Stoicism is demanding. It wants you to express your highest self at all times. It wants you to focus on what you control, and accept the rest with equanimity. It wants you to recognize your power to perceive events in constructive ways. And it wants you to take responsibility for your own flourishing.

The following 21 preparing practices and strategies will help you become the person who's ready to deal with life's challenges.

All these practices don't require any specific life situations. You can do them anytime, and almost anywhere. There are no excuses for not doing them. All they need are a few minutes of your time and some self-discipline.

You'll find different sorts of practices:

- Mindsets to adopt
- Visualization practices
- Writing practices
- Journaling practices
- Outdoor practices
- Lifestyle interventions

Ready, set, go!

Practice 1

The Stoic Art of Acquiescence: Accept and Love Whatever Happens

"O world, I am in tune with every note of thy great harmony.

For me nothing is early, nothing late, if it be timely for thee.

O Nature, all that thy seasons yield is fruit for me."

– MARCUS AURELIUS

Accept rather than fight every little thing that happens. We heard about Stoic acceptance in Chapter 3. If we resist reality, if we think things are going against us, if we fight with what is, then we will suffer. Therefore, we should not wish for reality to be different, but accept it as it is.

"If this is the will of nature, then so be it." That's a maxim the Stoics lived by. Today, we have the similar saying "Thy will be done." And it doesn't matter whether we call it God, Nature, Fortune, or Fate—but we must acknowledge that there's something bigger than us, and that we don't control everything that happens around us.

The art of acquiescence is about the willing acceptance of external events. Accept even what the majority of people would judge as "bad." Epictetus says that as philosophers we should adapt to whatever happens, so that nothing happens against our will and nothing that we wish for fails to happen. Bring your will into harmony with what's going on. "Fate leads the willing, and drags along the reluctant," as Seneca put it.

Remember the dog leashed to a cart metaphor? The dog can either enjoy the ride and run smoothly alongside the cart, or he can stubbornly resist the direction of the cart while being dragged behind anyway. If we resist what happens, then we get dragged behind just like that dog. That's called suffering.

It's much smarter to accept reality and focus on where our power lies. As we've seen earlier, the hallmark of an admirable poker player is that he plays the best regardless of his hands. In the end, not the one with the objectively best cards, but the one who plays his cards the best, wins.

You don't get to choose the hands you're dealt, only how you want to play them. Your hands in poker as in life are indifferent, learn to accept them *equally*, without judging. If you can do that, if you can accept rather than resist what happens, then you will no longer be dependent upon things being in a certain way.

Get this impressive example:

Aged 67, after another day at the lab, Thomas Edison returned home. After dinner, a man arrived at this house with urgent news: A fire had broken out at the research campus a few miles away.

Fire engines could not stop the fire. Fueled by chemicals, green and yellow flames shot up high in the sky, threatening to destroy the entire empire Edison had spent his life building.

When Edison made it to the scene, he immediately told his son, "Go get your mother and all her friends, they'll never see a fire like this again."

What a reaction, right? He lost much of what he'd been working on his whole lifetime, and instead of getting sad or angry, he accepted it and tried to make the best with it. He started rebuilding what the fire destroyed the next day. That's playing the cards well. That's nonresistance.

Plus, this example shows that Stoic acceptance has nothing to do with passive resignation. Edison started rebuilding everything the very next day. He accepted his fate graciously and tried to make the best with it. And that's what the Stoics advise us to do: Don't fight with reality, but bring your will into harmony with it, and focus on where your power lies.

Marcus Aurelius has a trick to bring his will into harmony with reality. He compares what happens to us to what a doctor prescribes to us. Just like you take some medicine when a doctor tells you to, we should take external events as they are, because they're like the medicine there to help us.

What happens to us is nature's treatment to become better people. Those things happen *for* us, not *against* us, even if it doesn't seem so.

Here's what helps me: Nature is immensely complex and it's impossible to tell whether anything that happens is good or bad. Because you never know what will be the consequences of misfortunes. And you never know what will be the consequences of good fortune. Therefore, I try to accept everything as if I had chosen it. This way, I move from a whiney victim to a responsible creator.

Practice 1

(I highly recommend you check out this 2-minute YouTube video: The Story of the Chinese Farmer.)

Practice 2

Undertake Actions with a Reserve Clause

"I will sail across the ocean, if nothing prevents me."

– SENECA

The *reserve clause* is a classic Stoic trick to maintain equanimity and tranquility. It will help you accept the outcomes of your actions. When you plan to do something, you add the caveat "if nothing prevents me."

Seneca defines the reserve clause with the formula, "I want to do such and such, as long as nothing happens which may present an obstacle to my decision." I'm going to do this, if fate will have it. I'll do my best but the outcome is ultimately not within my control. I can't be absolutely certain that it will come out as planned, but I'll try my best.

- I will sail across the ocean, if nothing prevents me.
- I will work out Monday and Thursday this week, fate permitting.
- I will hit the target, God willing.

You set out to do something with the attitude that the outcome is not within your control and you're willing to calmly accept that things may not turn out as planned. Other people assume that *of course* things will go well. And if not, they'll be resisting reality and suffering indefinitely.

As Stoics, we bake the reserve clause into everything we do and foresee that something may intervene and prevent our wished outcome. We don't promise success to us beforehand. Therefore, it'll be easier to accept failure, and we'll be faster to get up again. Plus, we'll gain confidence because we're not overly attached to the outcome.

With that detachment from the outcome, we'll be able to maintain our tranquility instead of getting frustrated even if we don't get the outcome we hoped for.

The reserve clause implies two points:

1. Do your very best to succeed . . .
2. . . . and simultaneously know and accept that the outcome is beyond your direct control.

This is a bulletproof way to maintain your confidence: (1) you try your best to succeed, (2) you know that the results are out of your control, (3) you're prepared to accept success and failure equally, and (4) you continue to live with areté, moment to moment.

That's the Stoic archer all over again. Focus on what you control, and take the rest as it happens. Focus on the process—effort, training, preparation—and be ready to accept the outcome with equanimity. The reserve clause helps with exactly that. If we add that caveat when we shoot our arrow, we're aware that the outcome isn't up to us and we're prepared to accept success and failure equally. We're only responsible to shoot as well as possible, but not for hitting the target, that's down to fate.

It comes down to this: Know that sometimes things will not go your way even if you do your best, and regardless of whether you deserved it or not. Don't confuse your aspirations with how the universe should turn out.

Practice 3

What Stands in the Way Becomes the Way

"The impediment to action advances actions.

What stands in the way becomes the way."

– MARCUS AURELIUS

"Undoubtedly one of history's most effective formulas for overcoming every negative situation." That's what Ryan Holiday says about Marcus Aurelius' formula you just read above. He continues, "A formula for thriving not just in spite of whatever happens but *because of it*."

Ryan Holiday based a whole book on this formula—*The Obstacle Is the Way*. The main idea is that difficulties and challenges in life are only obstacles if we make them so. It depends on how we look at those challenges—we can either see obstacles and get blocked, or we can see opportunities and make progress.

In every challenge lies an opportunity for growth. If we're aware of that, we can make sure that what impedes us— setbacks and struggles—will actually *empower* us. We expect struggles beforehand (remember the reserve clause from

Practice 2?) and know they'll present a blank block of marble to hone our skills.

In Stoicism, that's always a chance to practice some virtue: courage, humility, reason, justice, patience, self-discipline, and forgiveness. Nothing can prevent us from doing this. Virtue is always within our control, it's always possible to respond with virtue to any given situation. What stands in the way becomes the way. Just another chance to practice being the best you can be.

No matter what life throws at us, we have a choice: Will we be blocked by challenges, or will we fight through them? Either we shrink or we grow. The adversity presents a stepping stool to reach a higher level as a person. Without this opportunity, we can't grow and remain where we are.

Imagine a fire. Every obstacle gets consumed and used as fuel. If there's nothing standing in the way, the fire dies. You are that fire. Nothing really is an obstacle because they only feed you and make you stronger. Marcus Aurelius calls this ability to use obstacles for fuel "turning the obstacle upside down."

Whenever something gets in the way, use that obstacle to practice your most important goal—to live with areté, to express the highest version of yourself. Nothing can prevent you from doing this. You will continue to make progress, and there will always be new obstacles, *ahem*, opportunities presenting themselves. It's within your control to use them as fuel and practice your skills.

This all comes down to your perception. The same situation can either be perceived as a lead ball chained to your feet, or as wings growing out of your shoulder blades. How you interpret the challenge is crucial to your success of overcoming it. Ultimately, it's never the challenges that matter, but how you perceive them.

"If you are pained by any external thing, it is not this thing that disturbs you, but your own judgment about it. And it is in your power to wipe out this judgment now." Marcus Aurelius says that your judgment makes an event into an obstacle or an opportunity. It's up to you.

You can find an opportunity for growth in everything. You can always try to turn obstacles upside down and find a way to respond with virtue.

And hey, this isn't about wearing rose-tinted glasses. Terrible things happen, that's for sure. This is just showing that you always have a choice. Either you bury your head in the sand when things seem to turn against you, or you keep your head up and look for an opportunity to grow.

You'll get better over time and will you reach a point with immense inner tranquility where nothing can shake you—you'll be ready to deal effectively with whatever life throws at you.

Practice 4

Remind Yourself of the Impermanence of Things

"When giving your child or wife a kiss, repeat to yourself,
'I am kissing a mortal.'"
– EPICTETUS

Change is a universal law of nature. Things are changing constantly. Life is ephemeral—people we care about may be snatched from us in a snap, without warning. This is why Marcus Aurelius often reminds himself of the time as a river metaphor, in which everything flows past: "Think often on the swiftness with which the things that exist and that are coming into existence are swept past us and carried out of sight. For all substance is as a river in ceaseless flow, its activities ever changing and its causes subject to countless variations, and scarcely anything stable."

Things are in constant change, they flow past—new things come and flow past. Therefore, we should remind ourselves how precious our loved ones are—they may soon flow past, too. Let's appreciate what we have now because it might be gone tomorrow. Life is impermanent.

Keep in mind that you are lucky to be able to enjoy the things you have, and that your enjoyment might end abruptly, and that you might never be able to enjoy those things again. Learn to enjoy stuff and people without feeling entitled to them, without clinging.

With the river metaphor in mind, you reduce attachment to what you love, and you diminish the fear of things you're averse to. Because you're aware that all is in constant change, also the things you dislike. You generally reduce the perceived importance of external things.

Knowing that nothing lasts makes you less attached and it becomes easier to accept when things change or when you lose what you love. Epictetus reminds us that when we're attached to a thing like a crystal cup, we should keep in mind what it really is, so that we won't be disturbed when it breaks. He continues: "So should it be with persons; if you kiss your child, or brother, or friend . . . you must remind yourself that you love a mortal, and that nothing that you love is your very own; it is given you for the moment, not forever nor inseparably, but like a fig or a bunch of grapes at the appointed season of the year, and if you long for it in winter you are a fool. So too if you long for your son or your friend, when it is not given you to have him, know that you are longing for a fig in winter time."

The next time you say goodbye to a loved one, silently remind yourself that this might be your final parting. You'll be less attached to them and if you see them again, you'll appreciate it much more.

Many things that happen to us we cannot change. But we can adopt a noble spirit to bear up bravely with all the changes nature sends our way, and bring our will into harmony with reality.

When there are no figs, there are no figs.

Things are in constant change. Become aware of the smallness of this present moment when you're reading this. Whoop, and gone. Compare this moment to the whole day, to the whole week, to your whole lifespan. Things change, *you* change. Imagine all the people who lived before you. And all the people who will follow when you're gone. Broaden your perspective to the whole history of the human race . . .

See? Things come and go. Nothing lasts.

Practice 5

Contemplate Your Own Death

"I am not eternal, but a human being; a part of the whole, as
an hour is of the day. Like an hour I must come and,
like an hour, pass away."

– EPICTETUS

Things are impermanent. Enjoy what you love as long as you
have it. If nothing else, then your own death will end it.
There's nothing we fear more than our own death. This fear
is irrational, say the Stoics, nothing but rumors from the
living.

Because of that fear, we don't think about our own death.
Yes, others might die, but not us—we feel immortal. Yet
we're not. Beware, what happens to others can happen to
you, too.

We don't know how much longer our heart will keep
beating. And it's not up to us to decide. It's only up to us to
decide *how* we want to live *right now*. To get the most out of
life, the Stoics advise us to live as if today were our last day.

"Think of yourself as dead," says Marcus Aurelius, "you
have lived your life. Now take what's left and live properly."

Living as if it's our last day is *not* about living a frivolous lifestyle with drugs, blackjack, and hookers. It's about periodically reflecting on the fact that you will not live forever, you're mortal, and you might not wake up the next morning. Like an hour, you will pass away.

The goal is not to change your activities necessarily, but your state of mind while doing those activities. Contemplating your own death won't depress you, no, it will enhance your enjoyment of life. It will turn to your advantage. You won't take things for granted anymore, and appreciate every little thing much more. You will savor each and every moment. Because you're well aware that all these things had not been granted to you indefinitely.

Thinking of your own death helps you stop making random choices and wasting time on trifles. You're more aware of what you want to spend your time with. It focuses your mind on the truly important—on who you want to be in this world. It helps you live with areté, no matter what you've missed to this day. Life is now and you want to make the best of it by expressing your highest self in every moment.

The old Romans had a name for this: *Memento mori* (remember you are mortal). Keep that in front of your eyes and you will not only appreciate your life and loved ones more, but you will also get much more out of your days. Marcus Aurelius advises to remind you of this every morning: "When you arise in the morning, think of what a precious privilege it is to be alive—to breathe, to think, to enjoy, to love."

Practice 6

Consider Everything as Borrowed from Nature

"We have no grounds for self-admiration, as though we were surrounded by our own possessions; they have been loaned to us. We may use and enjoy them, but the one who allotted his gift decides how long we are to be tenants; our duty is to keep ready the gifts we have been given for an indefinite time and to return them when called upon, making no complaint: it is a sorry debtor who abuses his creditor."

– SENECA

Do you truly own anything?

Your car, laptop, cat? Your body, status, relationships? No, because all those things can be taken away in a second. You may work overtime and pay the price to own those things, and yet they can be gone anytime. Fate, bad luck, or death can dispossess you of them without prior notice.

Car? Stolen!—Money? Lost!—Cat? Ran away!—Wife? Died!—High status? Gone!

We're not prepared to deal with such losses. We think we own those things and only realize we *don't* once they're gone. And now it's incredibly hard to deal with it. We're devastated, lost, and drenched in tears.

Seneca says we can't handle such losses because we're unaware of the possibility to lose those things in the first place. We never think about bad events in advance and get caught by surprise. But how can we be so unaware?

It's ignorance.

In his consolation letter to Marcia, he asks how we can see so many funeral processions passing past our houses yet not think about death. So many funerals are sad, yet we're still convinced our kids will outlive us. Many rich people lose all their possessions, yet we don't think it could happen to us.

So many *Missing Garfield* flyers hang in the streets, yet we don't think our *Tiger* could get lost too. How can we see so much misfortune in the world around us and not think of it happening in our own lives?

We close our eyes. We ignore it. We think we're invincible. We take things for granted. This ignorance will cost us dearly, we will end up devastated and unable to cope.

This is why Seneca advises to think of everything as borrowed from nature. You don't own anything. Everything you think you own has been loaned to you temporarily. Not as a gift, but as something you'll need to return whenever the lender wants it back. And as Seneca says, "it is a sorry debtor who abuses his creditor."

Think of all you've got as borrowed: your best friend, spouse, kids, cat, health, status, car, and laptop. These things have been loaned to you. Be aware of that and anticipate that the lender will want those things back at an unknown time.

Then, misfortune will hit you with less force and you'll be able to deal with it more effectively.

In the end, we come with nothing, and go with nothing.

Practice 7

Negative Visualization: Foreseeing Bad Stuff

"It is precisely in times of immunity from care that the soul
should toughen itself beforehand for occasions of greater
stress, and it is while Fortune is kind that it should fortify
itself against her violence. In days of peace the soldier
performs maneuvers, throws up earthworks with no enemy in
sight, and wearies himself by unnecessary toil, in order that
he may be equal when it is necessary. If you would not have
a man flinch when the crisis comes,

train him before it comes."

– SENECA

Do you take precautions to prevent bad stuff from
happening?

Most certainly you do. I do, too. But no matter how hard
we try, some bad things will happen anyway. That's where
this powerful Stoic tool comes in handy. *Negative
visualization* is an imagination exercise in which you foresee

bad stuff. It prepares you to stay calm and deal effectively with whatever life will throw at you.

One important goal of the Stoics is to be able to remain calm and reflected even in the face of adversity. So that you can live by your values and express your highest version of yourself—rather than panic and go crazy.

This requires training. The Stoics used negative visualization to train themselves to maintain equanimity and cope well even in challenging situations. They prepared to soften the shock of reality and achieve greater tranquility, but also to rehearse the philosophy's core principles. To deepen their values.

Think of this thought training as *foresight*. Before you go out and do something, ask yourself:

- What could go wrong?
- What obstacle could pop up?
- Where could I face difficulties?

That's emotional resilience training. You prepare yourself to face tough situations beforehand, when things are good, so that you'll be ready when things turn bad. That's how you avoid devastation, as Ryan Holiday expressed beautifully: "Devastation—that feeling that we're absolutely crushed and shocked by an event—is a factor of how unlikely we considered that event in the first place."

By considering challenging situations to pop you, you prepare yourself so that you won't feel crushed and shocked by them *if* they happen. And you'll be able to be your best.

Basically, you visualize possible bad future scenarios in your head. Ask what could go wrong in advance, before you start a trip, launch a product, or go on a date. You imagine those negative things as if happening *right now*. As you see that bad stuff happening right now in your head, you try to stay calm and respond in the best way possible.

Attention: The term "negative visualization" can be misleading. As learned in the second corner of the Stoic Happiness Triangle, external things are neither good nor bad, but indifferent. That's actually the basis of this Stoic practice—no external misfortune can truly be bad because it's outside our control. Only our reaction to it can be good or bad, and that's what we train for, to be able to react well, with virtue.

One more thing: You might be wondering if *negative visualization is similar to the previous exercises*. And you're totally right. Reminding yourself of the impermanence of things, of your own mortality, and that everything you have is only borrowed, are all forms of negative visualization.

Now, let Seneca remind you that, "Fortune falls heavily on those for whom she's unexpected. The one always on the lookout easily endures."

Practice 8

Voluntary Discomfort

"But neither a bull nor a noble-spirited man comes to be what
he is all at once; he must undertake hard winter training, and
prepare himself, and not propel himself rashly into what is
not appropriate to him."

– EPICTETUS

Let's undertake some hard winter training. The Stoics took
negative visualization a step further, instead of only
visualizing bad stuff, they actually practiced it!

They advised to occasionally practice getting
uncomfortable in order to be better off in the future. The goal
isn't to punish yourself with a whip or something, the goal is
to train endurance and self-control. This training will quieten
your appetite for material possessions, increase the
appreciation for what you have, and prepare you to deal
effectively when uncomfortable situations actually arise.

Basically, you practice getting comfortable with what you
would now describe as uncomfortable.

Let's look at three forms of voluntary discomfort:

1. Temporary Poverty: Seneca recommends spending a few days a month to live as if impoverished, "Be content with the scantiest and cheapest food, with coarse and rough dress, saying to yourself the while: Is this the condition that I feared?"

Be creative with this idea: Drink only water for a day. Eat for less than $3 a day for a week. Try fasting for a day or two. Wear old and dirty clothes. Spend a month on a tight budget. If you're hardcore, spend a night under a bridge.

2. Get Yourself in Uncomfortable Situations: Take Cato the Younger as an example. He was a senator in the late Roman Republic and an avid student of Stoic philosophy. And he practiced voluntary discomfort like no other. He strolled around Rome in uncommon clothing so people laughed at him. He walked barefoot and bareheaded in heat and rain. And he put himself on a rationed diet.

You can do such things, too. For example, underdress for cold weather while knowing that you'll feel uncomfortably cold. Pretend your bed is full of spiders and sleep a night on the floor. Imagine there's no hot water and take a cold shower. Pretend your car isn't working and use public transport.

In the army, they know this sort of training and say: "If it ain't raining, it ain't training." Go for a toughness run *because* it's raining.

3. Purposefully Forgo Pleasure: Instead of getting in uncomfortable situations, just forgo pleasures. Pass up an opportunity to eat a cookie—not because it's unhealthy, but because you want to improve your self-control and experience some discomfort. Choose not to watch your favorite sports team's game. Or choose not to go partying with your friends.

This may sound anti-pleasure but it's actually training you to become the person who can do what others dread doing and resist doing what others can't resist doing.

Remember what Epictetus says, that you must undergo hard winter training to become who you want to be. Train now when it's still easy, and you'll be prepared for when it gets tough.

Again, this isn't about punishing yourself; it's about expanding your comfort zone, getting more comfortable in uncomfortable situations, and improving your self-discipline, resilience, and confidence. You train yourself to do the things that are tough. And you train yourself to say no to the things that are hard to say no to.

Lastly, this is not about eliminating all comfort from your life. Keep all the comfort you want—a cozy bed, delicious food, hot showers, warm clothes—just go without those things sometimes.

Practice 9

Prepare Yourself for the Day: The Stoic Morning Routine

"When you first rise in the morning tell yourself: I will encounter busybodies, ingrates, egomaniacs, liars, the jealous and cranks. They are all stricken with these afflictions because they don't know the difference between good and evil."

– MARCUS AURELIUS

One of the most advocated routines by the Stoics is to take time to look inward, examine, and reflect. Best times to do that? In the morning after rising and in the evening before you go to bed.

Epictetus advises to rehearse the day in the morning, and then review your progress in the evening. At daybreak, we should ask ourselves a few questions:

- What do I still lack in order to achieve freedom from negative emotions?
- What do I need to achieve tranquility?
- What am I? A rational being.

The idea is to get better each and every day. Get a step closer toward our goals. Also, we should remind ourselves of our *rational* nature so we don't (over-)identify with body, property, or reputation. We better aspire to greater reason and virtue, and meditate on our actions.

Marcus Aurelius proposes to remind yourself in the morning "of what a precious privilege it is to be alive – to breathe, to think, to enjoy, to love." And as seen in the opening quote, he wants us to prepare to meet challenging people later in the day. (See Negative Visualization, Stoic Practice 7).

Today and every day, you can almost be certain to meet someone who seems like a jerk. The question is: Will you be ready for it? If you prepare yourself in the morning, chances improve that you'll be ready to face challenging interactions with patience, forgiveness, understanding, and kindness.

To be clear: You do not prepare to be against the world, you prepare to act reasonably within a chaotic world where not everybody is as well prepared as you are. Marcus further reminds himself that those people who oppose him are akin to him, "not of the same blood or birth as me, but the same mind." And these relatives can neither harm him nor can he be angry with them, because we are made for cooperation.

Seneca reminds himself of the impermanence of things each morning: "The wise will start each day with the thought, 'Fortune gives us nothing which we can really own.' Nothing, whether public or private, is stable."

Whatever has been reared over the work of years can be destroyed within a few seconds. How many towns in Syria and Macedonia have been swallowed up by a single shock of earthquake? How often has this kind of devastation laid Cyprus in ruins?

"We live in the middle of things which have all been destined to die. Mortal have you been born, to mortals you have given birth. Reckon on everything, expect everything." *Memento mori* (remember you are mortal). This mental preparation in the morning will help you focus on the important things and you will be ready to meet difficulties with calmness, resilience, and patience.

Expect everything and be ready for anything—only so can you be your best at all times.

Morning preparation is crucial if you want to keep your calm and express your highest self even in the midst of a storm.

Modify the Stoics' morning routines to your liking; maybe you want to form a plan for the day or maybe you want to give yourself a pep talk, maybe you want to exercise, meditate, or journal, and maybe you want to sing under the shower. Feel free, just make sure to keep a regular morning routine.

Always remember: "Mortal have you been born, to mortals you have given birth. Reckon on everything, expect everything."

Practice 10

Review Your Day: The Stoic Evening Routine

"I make use of this opportunity, daily pleading my case at my own court. When the light has been taken away and my wife has fallen silent, aware as she is of my habit, I examine my entire day, going through what I have done and said. I conceal nothing from myself, I pass nothing by. I have nothing to fear from my errors when I can say: 'See that you do not do this anymore. For the moment, I excuse you.'"

– SENECA

Rehearse your day in the morning, review your progress in the evening. At the end of each day, sit down with your journal and review: What did you do? What did you well? What not so well? How could you improve?

Keep constant watch over yourself and put up each day for personal review. Just like Marcus Aurelius did with his *Meditations*. He sat down to reflect on the day to gain personal clarity, and he wrote entirely to himself, not the public. And yet we read it two thousand years later . . .

Seneca says if we want our minds to flourish, we must improve by asking questions such as:

- What bad habit have you put right today?
- Which fault did you take a stand against?
- In what respect are you better?

Seneca compares this self-examination as pleading his case each night at his own court. He judges his actions and tries to make sure to not make the same mistakes again. A good man, he says, is glad to receive advice, while a poor man resents any guidance.

Epictetus advises to ask similar questions before you go to bed to review your acts. Additionally, he asks what duties are left undone, to make sure you get to them the next day.

The nightly self-analysis will help you gain control over your negative emotions because you subconsciously know you'll be judged by night. So you can lessen your anger and other emotional reactions. Seneca says you will even sleep better.

Most importantly, the reflection routine will contribute to your mindfulness throughout the day. *Attention,* as the Stoics call it, is a prerequisite to practice Stoicism. If you want to express your highest self at all times, you must be aware of your actions. Otherwise you might slip and fall into reactivity. And you essentially give up being a philosopher because you don't know what you do. You are mind*less*.

This is why daily reflection routines are crucial in Stoic philosophy—if you don't know where you went wrong, how are you supposed to improve as a person? If you don't know how you want to behave in the world, how can you be your best?

For example, one evening you reflect that you reacted like a jerk in traffic when this other driver cut you off and you ranted and raved. Next time you find yourself in the same situation, and if you're mindful enough, you decide to do better and stay calm, patient, and forgiving.

This is a no-brainer. Take five minutes each night to consciously recall the events of the day and review your actions. What did you do well? What not so? Did something upset you? Did you experience anger, envy, fear? How could you improve next time?

Combined with a morning routine, this is the perfect self-improvement tool: Your mental preparation combined with self-analysis will lead to continuous learning and self-growth. Plus it will make you more mindful of your actions.

Personally, I do the *good, better, best* exercise. I ask myself three simple questions:

- **Good:** What did I do well today?
- **Better:** How could I improve? What could I do better?
- **Best:** What do I need to do if I want to be the best version of myself?

Attention: Always stay kind and forgiving to yourself. Show some self-compassion. You're trying your best, that's all you can do. And even if you don't feel well, that's normal, everybody struggles and experiences setbacks. Take this to heart: always be kind to yourself.

Practice 11

Keep a Role Model in Mind: Contemplate the Stoic Sage

"'We need to set our affections on some good man and keep him constantly before our eyes, so that we may live as if he were watching us and do everything as if he saw what we were doing.' This . . . is Epicurus' advice, and in giving it he has given us a guardian and a moral tutor—and not without reason, either: misdeeds are greatly diminished if a witness is always standing near intending doers."

– SENECA

Aspiring Stoics are ambitious people and want to express their highest self at all times. One strategy we can use is to contemplate a role model and measure ourselves against it. The Stoics either used Zeus, Socrates, or the ideal Sage as a role model. They would ask: "What would the Sage do?"

Now the Stoic Sage is the ideal yet hypothetical role model in Stoic philosophy. She's absolutely virtuous, wise, and good—a perfect human being. Her character is honorable and praiseworthy, and she lives a smoothly flowing life in perfect harmony with herself and whole nature.

This fictitious ideal gives us direction, structure, and consistency in our actions. As we want to make progress as good people, we might compare ourselves against this ideal by asking, "What would the Sage do?" This can help us make the best decisions in challenging situations.

This simple question is helpful because it brings a pause between stimulus and response. It brings awareness into the situation, which is the first step toward positive change. Asking what the Sage would do gains time and prevents us from reacting mindlessly. It enables us to stay at the steering wheel of our actions and choose our best possible response.

So, in the words of Seneca, "Choose someone whose way of life as well as words . . . have won your approval. Be always pointing him out to yourself either as your guardian or as your model. There is a need, in my view, for someone as a standard against which our characters can measure themselves. Without a ruler to do it against you won't make crooked straight."

Listen to Seneca and always keep a role model in mind—it doesn't need to be the Sage. You can *choose* who to learn from. It can be an idol like Roger Federer, a superhero like Batman, or just a person you admire like your mom or dad. Imagine this person to constantly be watching you and your actions. This will bring more awareness into your daily life and enable you to choose your actions more deliberately.

Learn more about your role model either in person or by reading books, listening to podcasts, or watching movies. Just keep them always ready at hand to be your best. You can wear jewelry that reminds you of them, put their photograph on your bed stand, or keep their quote in your wallet.

Learning from role models is a powerful way to work on your virtue. You can even modify this practice by asking more generally, what would the perfect mother/father/employee do? What would Jesus do? What would Buddha do?

Also, says Marcus, "Take a good hard look at people's ruling principle, especially of the wise, what they run away from and what they seek out."

Watch the wise and keep Seneca's words in mind: "Without a ruler to do it against you won't make crooked straight" (and we're all crooked)

.

Practice 12

Stoic Aphorisms: Keep Your "Weapons" Ready at Hand

"Doctors keep their scalpels and other instruments handy for
emergencies. Keep your philosophy ready too."

– MARCUS AURELIUS

The Stoics often summarized their main principles in
succinct statements. We've encountered some of them in this
book: Living with areté / living in agreement with nature / of
things some are in our power, and others are not / preferred
indifferents.

They're similar to modern maxims such as shit happens /
lies don't travel far / actions speak louder than words.

Now, why did the Stoics use such aphorisms?

They knew that our thoughts dye our character. As they
wanted to be the best they could be, they tried to counteract
irrational thoughts and judgments with opposing, rational
beliefs. They observed irrational thoughts popping up in their
minds and wanted to be ready so they could replace those
irrational thoughts with more positive and helpful ones.

That's where their aphorisms entered the game. In order to have positive beliefs ready at mind, they had to formulate their fundamental principles extremely simple and clear— precisely so that they were memorable and always remained accessible to the mind. That's the only way their principles could be applicable to the chaotic and rapidly-changing reality.

These laconic statements were used as reminders and aids in everyday life to guide behavior when in doubt. They can be thought of as "weapons" of the mind to fight off disturbing thoughts and judgments. Marcus Aurelius uses a distinct comparison: "The model for the application of your principles is the boxer rather than the gladiator. The gladiator puts down or takes up the sword he uses, but the boxer always has his hands, and needs only to clench them into fists."

Just like a boxer with his fists, try to have your principles ready at all times.

That's similar to Epictetus' *Enchiridion*: It's a tiny summary of the most important principles from the *Discourses*, and translates literally into "ready at hand"— always available to help you deal with life's challenges.

The Stoics were obviously interested in the practice of their principles, that's why they tried to compress them into memorable statements that could be used when needed most—out in the real world, when struggling. They wanted to make progress and actually apply what they learned in the classroom.

So, if you're anything like them, then create and memorize such easily accessible statements that remind you of how you want to behave in the world, and who you want to be. Ask: What are my core values? What do I want to stand for?

Know this: The statements you formulate will be indispensable weapons in the fight between you trying to be the best you can be and the hellfire of reality that gets in the way. Ultimately, these weapons decide upon life or death—a happy and smoothly flowing life or a miserable and unfulfilling one.

Practice 13

Play Your Given Roles Well

"Remember that you are an actor in a play determined by the author: if short, then short; if long, then long. If he wants you to act as a beggar, then act even that with excellence, just as a cripple, a ruler or a citizen. Because that is your objective: to act the role that is given to you well. To select the role is up to someone else."

– EPICTETUS

Each of us has different roles to play: a human being, a citizen of the world, a father or mother, son or daughter, brother or sister, husband or wife, friend or foe, teacher or pupil, neighbor or stranger, young or old. Some roles are natural like being a human being, a daughter, and sister. And some are acquired like being a wife and a teacher.

These roles are not the same for all of us. Even if both of us are sons; my father might be supportive and kind, and your father discouraging and aggressive. So our roles are different.

Now each of our roles has specific duties. Like an actress in a play, you must play your given role well, even if you don't like it. Act in a way that is consistent with your role. You're given the ability to use reason, and you're free to choose your actions, so you're able to play your role well.

Those roles often come in relations to one another. If you're a daughter, your role is to be a good daughter in relation to your parents. Your mother's role in relation to you is to be a good mother. Her role in relation to your father is to be a good wife.

Epictetus says that if you fulfill your duties toward others, then you're living in agreement with nature, which is the direct path to a happy and smoothly flowing life.

Focus on your side of the relations to others. It's possible that you're a great daughter, but your father isn't a great father, and he doesn't play his role well. That has nothing to do with you. You were given this role as a daughter and must play it well. You can only do your side of the relation. That's enough.

Fulfill your duties as a daughter even if your father doesn't fulfill his duties as a father to you. That's ultimately his loss, not yours. He's doing damage to himself by not living in harmony with nature. If he hurts you, he pays the price in a way or another. You might not see it at the moment, but he loses something by not fulfilling his duties. "No man is bad without suffering some loss," says Epictetus.

But if you try to hurt your father in return, then you don't fulfill your duties as a daughter and as a consequence injure yourself. You lose part of your character—the gentle, patient, and dignified.

Do you realize it? No. The loss of character is not accompanied by sickness or loss of possessions. You don't realize what you've lost—your gentle, patient, and dignified character.

This is a classic Stoic idea: Play your role well by being the best you can be, focusing on what you control, and ultimately being a good person.

"Reflect on the other social roles you play," Epictetus advises. "If you are a council member, consider what a council member should do. If you are young, what does being young mean, if you are old, what does age imply, if you are a father, what does fatherhood entail? Each of our titles, when reflected upon, suggests the acts appropriate to it."

Play your roles well, even if others don't.

Practice 14

Eliminate the Nonessential

"Most of what we say and do is not essential. If you can
eliminate it, you'll have more time, and more tranquility. Ask
yourself at every moment, 'Is this necessary?' But we need to
eliminate unnecessary assumptions as well. To eliminate
the unnecessary actions that follow."

– MARCUS AURELIUS

One thing that's certain is that the next moment is never
promised. And yet many people spend their days on things of
little value, wandering aimlessly in no clear direction,
mindlessly doing what comes easy—binge-watching Netflix,
chitchatting with coworkers, or following the latest celebrity
news.

We're unaware of the grains of sand trickling down from
our life-glass. We make random choices with no goals
whatsoever, until we wonder where our time went.

We must not let that happen. Instead, let's make no more
random actions. "Even the smallest thing should be done
with reference to an end," says Marcus Aurelius. As aspiring
Stoics, we must choose our actions wisely, spending our

grains of sand on what's important—and stop wasting our lives on trivial matters.

Let's banish the nonessential from our lives once and for all. And let's focus on the essential instead. This ability to cut through the extraneous and concentrate on the things that matter is immensely powerful. Find out for yourself how much more you can accomplish if you cut through the jungle of unimportance and focus on the spring of importance.

"If you seek tranquility, do less . . . do what's essential." This will bring a double satisfaction, says Marcus Aurelius, "to do less, better."

Ask yourself, "What are the most important things in my life?"

Once you know what those things are, you need to prioritize them. And eliminate what didn't make the list. This will gain you time and tranquility. Like everybody else, you have 24 hours in a day. And you choose how to spend those hours.

The Stoic Sage finds clarity in what's essential and will always focus on that. She's well aware that, every second, grains of sand are trickling away and cannot be brought back.

Practice 15

Forget Fame

"People who are excited by posthumous fame forget that the people who remember them will soon die too. And those after them in turn. Until their memory, passed from one to another like a candle flame, gutters and goes out."

– MARCUS AURELIUS

We're better off if we're indifferent to fame and social status. After all, it's not within our control.

What do others think of us? Not up to us. We must not mistake outward success with what's truly valuable—patience, confidence, self-control, forgiveness, perseverance, courage, and reason.

By seeking social status, we give other people power over us. We have to act in a calculated way to make them admire us, and we must refrain from doing things in their disfavor. We enslave ourselves by seeking fame.

Let's rather focus on what we control—our voluntary behavior. Being the best we can be is what matters. Expressing our highest self in every moment. We shouldn't seek thanks or recognition for doing the right thing. Doing the right thing is its own reward.

"When you've done well and another has benefited by it, why like a fool do you look for a third thing on top?" asks Marcus Aurelius. Instead of tying our well-being to what others think, we should tie it to our own actions. That's all we control.

Your character and your behavior is what matters. That way you will do what's right rather than what pleases others. Often, these are very different things. Get satisfaction from being your best. Forget about chasing fame and applause, focus on your virtuous behavior: acting with reason, courage, justice, and self-discipline.

Fame might come as a bonus from being a good person. But don't do it for the fame—it's uncertain, short-lived, and superfluous, as Marcus observes: "Consider the lives led once by others, long ago, the lives to be led by others after you, the lives led even now, in foreign lands. How many people don't even know your name. How many will soon have forgotten it. How many offer you praise now—and tomorrow, perhaps, contempt. That to be remembered is worthless. Like fame. Like everything."

Things almost change as you look at them, and then they will be forgotten.

Let's be indifferent to what others think of us. Let's be as dismissive of their approval as we are of their disapproval. And let's focus on where our power lies—our well-intended actions. Doing the right thing is its own reward. Let's find satisfaction in that.

Practice 16

Like a Minimalist: Live Simple

"Is it not madness and the wildest lunacy to desire so much
when you can hold so little?"

– SENECA

What are clothes for? Musonius Rufus advises to dress to protect our bodies, not to impress other people. Seek the necessary, not the extravagant. The same is true for our housing and furnishings. They should be functional and do little more than keep out heat and cold, and shelter us from the sun and wind.

Seneca likewise says that it makes no difference whether the house is built of turf or imported marble: "What you have to understand is that thatch makes a person just as good as a roof of gold does."

The Stoics favor a simple lifestyle—a lifestyle that fits our needs. And we should always keep in mind that material things are indifferent. What matters is how we handle them. For one thing, we should not get attached to what can be taken away. As Marcus reminds us, "Receive without pride, let go without attachment."

We should not hoard stuff. Most is useless and superfluous. We look at things as they're for free because they come cheap or as gifts, but they cost us dearly. Seneca makes the point that there's a hidden cost to all accumulating.

More is not always better. Free is not always free.

And once we experience luxury, we'll long for even more. Getting stuff won't make us happy, and we'll want more and more in order to quench our thirst. However, as Epictetus observes, "Freedom is not achieved by satisfying desire, but by eliminating it."

True wealth lies in wanting less. "No person has the power to have everything they want," Seneca says, "but it is in their power not to want what they don't have, and to cheerfully put to good use what they do have." Our goal should be to "seek riches, not from Fortune, but from ourselves."

Let's keep in mind that living by values such as mutual respect, trustworthiness, and self-control are more valuable than wealth or external success. We should never compromise our character to become wealthy. Being a good person is the highest good there is. And it's all that's needed to live a happy and fulfilling life.

But what if you are wealthy? Like Seneca and Marcus Aurelius were? First of all, wealth must come honorably and be spent honorably, says Seneca, and adds: "The wise man does not consider himself unworthy of any gifts from Fortune's hands: he does not love wealth but he would rather have it; he does not admit it into his heart but into his home, and what wealth is his he does not reject but keeps, wishing it to supply greater scope for him to practice his virtue."

Wealth often comes as a bonus if we act well and express our highest self. And if we do get it, then we should accept it without pride but also without clinging to it. It's good to have it and you can enjoy it, but you must be prepared to let it go. Whether you have it or not shouldn't make a difference. Seneca further says, "The influence of wealth on the wise person . . . is like a favorable wind that sweeps the sailor on his course."

The idea is to be able to enjoy something and at the same time be indifferent to it. So accept that favorable wind when you get it, but be indifferent or even happy if you don't get it. Ultimately, reality is good as it is—favorable winds and storms alike.

"Stoic philosophy calls for plain living, but not for penance," as author William Irvine puts it. It doesn't ask to renounce wealth. It does ask, however, to use it thoughtfully and keep in mind that it's only borrowed from Fortune and can be taken away any moment.

(As a side note: The Stoic philosophers didn't have the same opinion on this issue: Musonius Rufus and Epictetus thought luxurious living must be completely avoided because it corrupts us, while Seneca and Marcus Aurelius thought it's possible to live in a palace without being corrupted.)

Practice 17

Take Back Your Time: Cut Out News and Other Timewasters

"It is essential for you to remember that the attention you
give to any action should be in due proportion to its worth,
for then you won't tire and give up, if you aren't busying
yourself with lesser things beyond what should be allowed."
– MARCUS AURELIUS

Time cannot be brought back. Once the grain of sand trickles down our life-glass, it's gone forever.

Despite its value, people hand over their time freely to passersby, to screens of any kind, and other nonessential activities. "We're tight-fisted with property and money," says Seneca, "yet think too little of wasting time, the one thing about which we should all be the toughest misers."

Let's not spend our time on things that don't matter. Because the more time we spend on something, the more importance we give it. At the same time, what truly matters—family, friends, commitments, expressing the highest self—becomes less important because we spend less time on them.

By spending time on something, you give it importance.

We must be aware of where our time goes. The simplest way to find out? Measure your time!

We need to set priorities and spend the lion's share of our time on what matters. We need to say *no* to nonessential things. We must give up things we've been doing for a long time, unaware that they don't matter much. Just because we've been doing something for all our life doesn't mean we need it. Hear out Seneca: "Until we have begun to go without them, we fail to realize how unnecessary many things are. We've been using them not because we needed them but because we had them . . . One of the causes of the troubles that beset us is the way our lives are guided by the example of others; instead of being set to rights by reason we're seduced by convention."

Use reason rather than convention to choose what to spend your time on. The first thing to cut out is the news. "There is only one way to happiness," says Epictetus, "and that is to cease worrying about things which are beyond the power of our will." News is all about worrying about stuff outside our control. If you want to make progress as a person, then skipping the news is the perfect start. We only have a limited amount of time and energy, and news is not something an aspiring Stoic chooses to spend it on.

"If you wish to improve, be content to appear clueless or stupid in extraneous matters—don't wish to seem knowledgeable." Epictetus reminds us it's ok to appear clueless in nonessential matters such as the latest celebrity scandal or Super Bowl winner.

Look, the media broadcasts everything as super important. But what's a scandal today won't even be covered again tomorrow . . . Let's just be aware that not every headline is important, we won't miss out. On the contrary, we risk wasting our time, as Seneca observes: "It is not that we have a short time to live, but that we waste a lot of it. Life is long enough, and a sufficiently generous amount has been given to us for the highest achievements if it were all well invested. But when it is wasted in heedless luxury and spent on no good activity, we are forced at last by death's final constraint to realize that it has passed away before we knew it was passing."

Don't let that happen. Actively choose where to spend your time and energy. It's not just the news that's stealing your time, other timewasters are dangerous, too.

Video games, TV series, funny fail videos, and other superficial activities are the most common. We're all guilty and the Stoics don't ask to cut it out completely, just to be aware of your time passing by, and spending it mindfully.

Make sure you won't be the old person with no other evidence besides your age and white hair to prove you've lived a long life. Take back your time and protect it like a mother protects her child. Focus on the things that matter and stop wasting time on things that don't.

Seneca has the last words on this: "Even if you had a large part of your life remaining before you, you would have to organize it very economically to have enough for all the things that are necessary; as things are, isn't it the height of folly to learn inessential things when time's so desperately short!"

Practice 18

Win at What Matters

"You are winning affection in a job in which it is hard to
avoid ill-will; but believe me it is better to understand the
balance-sheet of one's own life than of the corn trade."

– SENECA

His father-in-law lost his position as person in charge of
Rome's granary when Seneca sent him this reminder that it's
not too bad.

Who cares? Says Seneca, now he can spend time with
what's truly important, "The love and practice of the virtues,
forgetfulness of the passions, the knowledge of how to live
and die, and a life of deep tranquility."

It's more important to understand the balance-sheet of
one's own life than that of the corn market, stock market, or
our office.

But what do we do? We invest our working time in
getting better at topics necessary for our (future) jobs, and
our leisure time in mindless activities to numb ourselves.

We become experts at fantasy series, video games, sports,
celebrity news, and effortless jobs—unaware that none of

these things will teach us anything about how to listen to our friends, how to become self-disciplined, and what to do with anger or grief.

We confuse getting better at stuff with learning how to live, and how to be a good person.

"At the end of your time on this planet," Ryan Holiday asks you, "what expertise is going to be more valuable—your understanding of matters of living and dying, or your knowledge of the '87 Bears? Which will help your children more—your insight into happiness and meaning, or that you followed breaking political news every day for thirty years?"

Wow, right? It's clear what's more valuable. So let's actually use this understanding and set the right priorities and make sure we invest in what truly matters.

There's nothing harder to learn than how to live, says Seneca. It's about time to get started. Forget about acing tests, climbing the career ladder, and learning everything about cryptocurrency—what's the point of winning at those things but losing in the game of being a good mother, sister, and friend?

Look, there's definitely time and space for those things, but not at the cost of improving as a person. That's what we've just decided to be more valuable.

Don't envy the colleagues who shine bright at the office, as their success comes at the cost of life. The father who puts in eighty hours a week might be a hero at work, but he probably neglects his wife, son, and health.

Successful is a broad term. This father might have been employee of the last three months, but in this time he never listened to his wife, never saw his son's soccer games, and he was cranky due to his sleep deprivation.

Again, what's the point of winning at a career but losing at the effort to be a good husband and father?

Let's get better at what matters. Let's learn how to deal with depressive thoughts, how to be a good listener, how to stay calm in the face of adversity, and how to be a good spouse, parent, and friend.

That's our inward transformation nobody knows about. And it's much more important than the superficial outward transformation. Who you truly are inwardly is way more important than who people believe you to be.

Your most valuable asset is your character.

It will help you win at what matters.

Practice 19

Become an Eternal Student

"Leisure without study is death—a tomb

for the living person."

– SENECA

As an aspiring Stoic philosopher, you're by definition a lover of wisdom. You love to learn about how to live—you're a seeker of wisdom.

Remember, the Stoics saw themselves as veritable *warriors of the mind*—to learn how to live and most importantly, to put it into practice. Epictetus taught his students to contemplate their lives as if they were at a festival—the festival of life.

This metaphor conveys a sense of gratitude for life because it's a reminder that life will soon come to an end. Plus, seeing life as a festival helps us regard the turmoil of life in a more detached manner—just like a busy and chaotic festival.

Now, as philosophers, we should seek to study the festival before we leave it, and suck in as much knowledge as possible. It's our duty to make progress as the festival goes on. Day after day. As Seneca says, "leisure without study is death."

"Make sure you enjoy your relaxation like a poet—not idly but actively, observing the world around you, taking it all in, better understanding your place in the universe," as Ryan Holiday puts it. "Take a day off from work every now and then, but not a day off from learning."

We shall not only leave the remnants of time to learning, but we must actively make time for it. That's what we're here for. To seek wisdom to improve ourselves, to get better, to learn how to be a good parent, spouse, and friend.

"The value of education (knowledge) like that of gold is valued in every place," says Epictetus.

You don't have an excuse. Today it's easier than ever to learn something new every day. Wisdom is abundant all over the internet. Books are cheap and get delivered to your reading chair. We can learn from the smartest people who ever lived—for a few bucks.

As an avid student, keep in mind two things:

1. Be humble: As Epictetus teaches us, "It is impossible to learn that which one thinks one already knows." And Marcus adds, "If anyone can prove and show to me that I think and act in error, I will gladly change it—for I seek the truth."

2. Put it into practice: Don't be satisfied with mere learning, Epictetus warns us, "For as time passes we forget and end up doing the opposite." As warriors of the mind, we must go out and actually live out what we've learned.

Practice 20

What Do You Have to Show for Your Years?

"Nobody works out the value of time: men use it lavishly as if it cost nothing. But if death threatens these same people, you will see them praying to their doctors . . . you will see them prepared to spend their all to stay alive . . . We have to be more careful in preserving what will cease at an unknown point."

– SENECA

We forget we're mortal.

We live as if we're going to live forever. Until we realize we're not. And that's when we wish we had started earlier to actually live.

People are prepared to give everything to stay alive. But when they are alive, they squander their time. Unaware that it will cease any moment.

"You are living as if destined to live forever, your own frailty never occurs to you; you don't notice how much time has already passed, but squander it as though you had a full and overflowing supply—though all the while that day which you are devoting to somebody or something may be your last. You act like mortals in all that you fear, and like immortals in all that you desire."

This last sentence, that we act like mortals in everything we fear and like immortals in all we desire—it's been true for me. And I'm considered a person who's been taking many risks. Building a business, quitting a secure job, selling everything, moving abroad, and trying to write a book.

And still I feel fear is holding me back. And still I feel there will be enough time for the things I truly want to do. I guess that's a human thing to do.

But if we're aware of it, if we know about this tendency to behave as we're going to live forever, we can remind ourselves of our mortality, we can counter steer, even do what we fear, and make sure we purposefully fill up our years with great experiences.

It's not about *not* playing video games, *not* watching TV, *not* working full-time—it's about the awareness and purposefulness we bring into these things. We can still choose to do whatever we think is worth spending our time with.

Let's ask ourselves, though: Do we spend our time with what we think is right? Or are we going to be the person praying to the doctor, willing to give all we have for a few more months?

Are we going to be the person not ready to die when it's time? Thinking there are so many more things we wanted to do in our time alive? Full of regrets of what we've missed?

If you look back now at your life, have you lived sufficiently? What do you have to show for your years? What else do you want to experience? Who do you want to be in this world?

I want to make sure that I can look back and say: "Yes, I made the most of it. I lived well. I savored every drop of my life." It's not about trophies and status, but about making progress as a person, growing into a mature human being, thriving in my deep values of calm, patience, justice, kindness, perseverance, humor, courage, and self-discipline.

The best possible self I see in my imagination—I want to spend my days living up to this ideal, trying to be as good as I can be, so that I get as close to it as possible.

I want to make the best with my waking hours. Well aware that life can be taken away at a snap.

The Stoics say it's not about the years you live, but about how you live those years. As Cato the Younger put it beautifully: "The value of good health is judged by its duration, the value of virtue is judged by its ripeness."

"It's possible," Seneca adds, "for a person who has had a long life to have lived too little."

Let's make sure we spend our time wisely so that we can look back with a content smile rather than a regretful sigh.

Practice 21

Do What Needs to Get Done

"On those mornings you struggle with getting up, keep this thought in mind—I am awakening to the work of a human being. Why then am I annoyed that I am going to do what I'm made for, the very things for which I was put into this world? Or was I made for this, to snuggle under the covers and keep warm? It's so pleasurable. Were you then made for pleasure? In short, to be coddled or to exert yourself?"

– MARCUS AURELIUS

Even Marcus, the one who's teaching us so much, often struggled to get up in the morning. Even he procrastinated. Even he didn't feel great all the time.

But he worked on it. And he got himself to do what's necessary.

We're not born for pleasure, he says. Just look at the plants, birds, ants, spiders, and bees—they go about their individual tasks. Do you hear them moan and complain? Nope, they do what they do, as best as they can. Day in, day out.

But we human beings are not willing to do our jobs? We feel lazy. Unmotivated. Sluggish. There is certainly time to sleep and rest, but there's a limit to that. "And you're over the limit," Marcus reminds himself. But he hasn't done all his work yet. He's still below his quota.

And we are, too. It's time to get up and do what we must. We won't live forever, as Seneca reminds us: "How late it is to begin really to live just when life must end! How stupid to forget our mortality, and put off sensible plans to our fiftieth and sixtieth years, aiming to begin life from a point at which few have arrived!"

"Putting things off is the biggest waste of life," Seneca says, "it snatches away each day as it comes, and denies us the present by promising the future. The greatest obstacle to living is expectancy, which hangs upon tomorrow and loses today. You are arranging what lies in Fortune's control, and abandoning what lies in yours . . . The whole future lies in uncertainty: live immediately."

So let's live immediately and not procrastinate any longer.

"Enough of this miserable, whining life. Stop monkeying around!" Marcus shows us how to take responsibility for our own lives. He wants to be at the steering wheel. As the Emperor, he needs to get things done.

And we're Emperors, too. Emperors of our own lives! We inherently know what to do. We just don't feel like it. Something inside is holding us back. We must keep in mind, though, that it's the successful among us who do what needs to get done whether they feel like it or not.

They know they're responsible for their own flourishing and choose to suffer a little every day rather than a lot whenever they realize they're not making any progress whatsoever.

That's self-discipline. That's dealing effectively with the negative feelings trying to hold us back.

Acknowledge the inner resistance and do it anyway. You're strong enough to get up in the morning even when tired. You're disciplined enough to resist that cookie even when attracted. You're courageous enough to help the stranger even when scared.

It's time to be the person you want to be. Today, not tomorrow.

At the end of the day, we get what we deserve.

Stop monkeying around, live immediately!

Chapter 7

Situational Practices

How to Deal with Yourself when Life Gets Tough?

When life is going smoothly, it's easy to live by the Stoic principles. It's when life kicks and punches you that it gets much harder.

As Mike Tyson said, "Everybody has a plan until they get punched in the face." Now, as aspiring Stoics, it's exactly in those moments when we need to remain calm, step back from our impulses, and consciously choose the smartest response.

Remember, it's not what happens to us, but our reactions to it that matter. We get disturbed not by the event itself, but by our interpretation of the event.

Life doesn't go smoothly. It's meant to be challenging and it'll throw nasty stuff at you:

- You will lose what you love
- You will get sick
- You will face critical life decisions
- Your favorite mug will break
- You will feel miserably depressed for no reason
- The world will seem to be against you

Life gets tough. The following practices and strategies will help you deal with it effectively.

Practice 22

Your Judgment Harms You

"If you are pained by any external thing, it is not this thing
that disturbs you, but your own judgment about it. And it is
in your power to wipe out this judgment now."
– MARCUS AURELIUS

You are disturbed not by what happens, but by your opinion
about it. That's a classic Stoic principle. Your troubled mind
comes from judging an outside event as undesirable or bad.
Often in the form of whining, moaning, and complaining
about it.

Keep that in mind: Nothing but opinion is the cause of a
troubled mind.

Harm does not come from what happens—an annoying
person or unloved situation—but from your reaction to it.
Your harm comes from your belief about the event. So when
someone pushes your buttons, it's not this person, but your
interpretation that hurts you.

It's your opinion that fuels the negative feelings.

Your reaction decides whether harm has occurred or not.
Marcus Aurelius says it needs to be this way, because

otherwise other people would have power over you. And that's not in the universe's intention. Only you have access to your mind, only you can ruin your life.

Take responsibility. Otherwise, I could write here that you're a jerk and you'd be harmed no matter what. But I don't have this power over you. If you get hurt by my words, then it's your interpretation, not my words that harm you.

It's crazy if we think about it: The interpretation of a remark has such an immense power. It's the difference between a face covered by a smile or drenched in tears. You basically have the power to get fueled by name-calling. If you interpret these words in a positive way, then you draw power from them.

It's your judgment that hurts you. And it's your judgment that empowers you. I remember some soccer star saying something along the lines of, "The whistling and booing by the opposing fans whenever I have the ball, that motivates me."

While another player might get hurt and loses focus, this one gets fueled by it.

Now the next time you're disturbed by something, remember that it's your judgment about the situation that hurts you. Try to remove the judgment, and the hurt will vanish, too. Don't judge the event as good or bad, just take it as it is—and you won't get harmed.

It's your reaction that shows whether you've been harmed or not. As Marcus Aurelius puts it: "Choose not to be harmed—and you won't feel harmed. Don't feel harmed—and you haven't been."

It's obviously not easy, but it's good to know none the less.

Just try this: Don't whine, moan, or complain.

Practice 23

How to Deal With Grief

"It's better to conquer grief than to deceive it."

– SENECA

A friend of mine committed suicide a few years ago. It's still hard to understand, but I've overcome the grief that accompanied me for a long time. You may know this feeling.

The Stoics are stereotyped as suppressing their emotions, but that's mistaken. Their philosophy intends to deal with emotions immediately rather than running away from them.

Running away is hard anyway, because we cannot help but feel grief-stricken when we learn about the sudden death of a loved one. That's like an emotional reflex. "Nature requires from us some sorrow," says Seneca. And he adds that, "more than this is the result of vanity."

Some grief is required. Proper grief according to Seneca is when our reason "will maintain a mean which will copy neither indifference nor madness, and will keep us in the state that is the mark of an affectionate, and not an unbalanced, mind."

We should let the tears flow, but let them also cease. And we can sigh deeply as long as we stop at some point. Because

175

at some point the consequences of grief are more harmful than what aroused it in the first place, says Marcus Aurelius.

As they say, if you find yourself in a hole, stop digging. Face the emotion, and get out of the hole. At some point the negative feeling will feed from itself, like a vicious cycle. You feel bad about still being grief-stricken, this will make you feel worse, and so on. You will keep on digging and never find out of the hole.

One thing we can do is to think about how much worse off we'd be if we had never been able to enjoy the company of the person who passed away. Rather than mourning the end of her life, we could be grateful for the moments we experienced together. This may make us sad, but also grateful.

For Seneca, the best weapon against grief is reason, because "unless reason puts an end to our tears, fortune will not do so."

For example, the person you grieve over, would she have wanted you to be tortured with tears? If yes, then she's not worthy of your tears and you should stop crying. If no, and if you love and respect her, then you should stop crying.

Also remember that things don't happen against you. So remove your sense of having been wronged. You haven't. The universe isn't against you.

That's terribly hard in moments of great sorrow, but it's really not reasonable to grieve for too long. Life goes on. Also, as proper Stoic students, we already prepared for this to happen when we engaged in negative visualization (Practice 7) and contemplated on the impermanence of things (Practice 4).

What to do when others grieve?

Epictetus says we should be careful not to "catch" the grief of others. We should sympathize with the person and if appropriate even accompany her moaning with our own. In doing so, be careful not to moan inwardly.

"We should display signs of grief without allowing ourselves to experience grief," as William Irvine puts it. He goes on, "If a friend is grieving, our goal should be to help her overcome her grief. If we can accomplish this by moaning insincerely, then let us do so. For us to 'catch' her grief, after all, won't help her but will hurt us."

It's not really "moaning insincerely" if you know the feeling and feel with her. You're trying to help without getting in danger yourself. There's nothing wrong with that, and I mean you don't need to cry your eyes out. Just be there and let her know you understand, and it's alright to be sad.

It's as they tell you each time you board a plane, "Put your oxygen mask on first." As you cannot help anyone when you're dead, and you cannot help others when you're as grief-stricken as they are.

Practice 24

Choose Courage and Calm over Anger

"Keep this thought handy when you feel a fit of rage coming on—it isn't manly to be enraged. Rather, gentleness and civility are more human, and therefore manlier. A real man doesn't give way to anger and discontent, and such a person has strength, courage, and endurance—unlike the angry and complaining. The nearer a man comes to a calm mind, the closer he is to strength."

– MARCUS AURELIUS

Anger is a *passion*, a negative emotion the Stoics want to minimize. Seneca's essay *On Anger* is the best source of Stoic advice on anger.

Anger, the desire to repay suffering, is brief madness, says Seneca. Because an angry man lacks self-control, is forgetful of kinship, is deaf to reason and advice, gets aroused by trifles, and doesn't know what's true and false—

"very like a falling rock which breaks itself to pieces upon the very thing which it crushes."

Getting angry will hurt yourself the most. And its damage is enormous: "No plague has cost the human race more." That's why the best plan is to reject straightway the first signs of anger and resist its beginnings. Because once we get carried away by anger, reason counts for nothing, anger will do as much as it chooses, and it'll be hard to turn it off.

Although we cannot control our initial reaction, if we're aware enough, we can decide to go along or not. Anger, then, is a form of judgment. We interpret the situation in a way that we decide it's ok to get angry.

But "of what use is anger," asks Seneca, "when the same can be arrived at by reason?"

Anger is prone to rashness. Reason is more trustworthy because it's considered and deliberate. "Reason wishes to give a just decision; anger wishes its decision to be thought just."

"The sword of justice is ill-placed in the hands of an angry man."

Anger is not useful, "No man becomes braver through anger, except one who without anger would not have been brave at all: anger does not therefore come to assist courage, but to take its place." We can find sufficient inducement without anger—with the right values in place such as love, compassion, justice, and courage.

Instead of being led by dangerous and unpredictable anger, we're motivated by intrinsic values, and deliberately choose to do the right thing.

"When a man is wandering about our fields because he has lost his way, it is better to place him on the right path than to drive him away." Seneca makes this beautiful comparison. He says we should not hunt down the people who have lost their ways and err in their actions, but show them the right course. Instead of reacting to anger with anger, we better choose a more sensible and compassionate way, and try to help them.

Instead of impulsively getting angry, take a deep breath and deliberately choose to stay calm. This calm will not only rob misfortune of its strength, but also empower you to act in a just and courageous way. As Marcus says, "The nearer a man comes to a calm mind, the closer he is to strength."

Generally, we shouldn't give circumstances the power to rouse anger. The circumstances don't care at all. It's like getting mad at something far bigger than us. It's like taking something personally that doesn't care about us. Things don't happen against us, they just happen.

Getting angry at a situation doesn't have an impact on the situation. It doesn't change it, it doesn't improve it. Oftentimes, what angers us doesn't really harm us, and our anger will outlast the damage done to us.

We're being fools when we allow our tranquility to be disrupted by trifles. That's why Marcus recommends contemplating the impermanence of the world around us. What angers us now will be forgotten tomorrow.

When you're angry, says Seneca, take steps to turn anger's indications into their opposites: Force yourself to relax your face, take a deep breath, soften your voice, and slow your pace of walking—your internal state will soon resemble your external, relaxed state.

You can also try to describe the situation making you angry as dispassionately and objectively as possible, explains Epictetus. This will gain you time and help you see the situation with greater distance.

And he says we should always keep in mind that it's not the situation that harms us, but our interpretation about it. "So when someone arouses your anger, know that it's really your opinion fueling it."

So, instead of being angry all the time and torment the lives of those around you, why not "make yourself a person to be loved by all while you live and missed when you have made your departure?" Seneca asks.

Practice 25

Beat Fear with Preparation and Reason

"We are more often frightened than hurt; and we suffer more
from imagination than from reality."

– SENECA

What we fear will often not happen in reality. But our
imaginary fear has real consequences. We're held back by
our fears, we're paralyzed by what isn't real.

The Stoics know about the danger of fear. The actual
damage of what we fear pales in comparison to the damage
done by ourselves as we're blindly trying to prevent what we
fear.

The primary cause of fear, says Seneca, is that "instead of
adapting ourselves to present circumstances we send out
thoughts too far ahead." It's a projection to the future about
something we don't control that causes a dangerous amount
of worry.

We want something that's not under our control, as
Epictetus explains wonderfully: "When I see a man in a state
of anxiety, I say, 'What can this man want?' If he did not

want something which is not in his power, how could he still be anxious? It is for this reason that one who sings to the lyre is not anxious when he is performing by himself, but when he enters the theatre, even if he has a very good voice and plays well: for he not only wants to perform well, but also to win a great name, and that is beyond his own control."

We fear because we want what's outside our power, or we're too attached to something that's not in our power to keep. We're attached to people we love and fear losing them. We're attached to the security of a regular salary. And we desire what's not in our power to receive.

We must stop attaching ourselves to external things and desires which are not under our control. Because a lack of control leads to fear.

He who does not desire anything outside his control cannot be anxious.

"The man who has anticipated the coming of troubles takes away their power when they arrive," says Seneca. That's why it's so important to prepare for challenging situations to arise.

Anticipating calamities is not about ruining the present moment, but optimizing it. We'll be less afraid of things which might never happen. The Stoics think the best path to freedom is by imagining what we fear as it's going to happen and examining it in our mind—until we can view it with detachment.

The common way to deal with fear is to hide from it and trying to think of something else. But this is probably the worst technique of all. Fear grows by not being looked at.

The proper way to deal with what we fear is thinking about it rationally, calmly, and often—until it becomes familiar. You'll get bored with what you once feared, and your worries will disappear. By confronting your fears, whether in imagination or in reality, you reduce the stress caused by those fears.

Marcus has another way of dealing with fear: "Clear your mind and get a hold on yourself and, as when awakened from sleep and realizing it was only a bad dream upsetting you, wake up and see that what's there is just like those dreams."

What you fear is often a product of your imagination, not reality. You're afraid of something not because the reality of it is bad, but because you think reality would be bad. Most people who are afraid of spiders have never even been touched by one. What do they fear?

We fear in imagination. It's like a dream. Instead of going along mindlessly, we must stop and ask rationally: "Does this make any sense?"

We're creating nightmares for ourselves. That's why we must wake up and stop this madness. We get upset at dreams. What causes the fear isn't real, but the consequences are very much real and get in our way. We're the ones holding us back.

Look, you can't cure all your fears all at once. But if we manage to get less attached to things, realize that what we fear is in our imagination, and if we face our fears even in imagination only, then we can overcome most of our fears. Step by step.

Practice 26

Blame Your Expectations

"The cucumber is bitter? Then throw it out. There are
brambles in the path? Then go around them. That's all you
need to know. Nothing more. Don't demand to know 'why
such things exist.' Anyone who understands the world will
laugh at you, just as a carpenter would if you seemed
shocked at finding sawdust in his workshop, or a shoemaker
at scraps of leather left over from work."

– MARCUS AURELIUS

We get angry, sad, or disappointed because reality doesn't
meet our expectations. We get surprised because things are
not as wished.

When you find yourself frustrated, don't blame other
people or outside events, but yourself and your unrealistic
expectations. Turn your focus inward, remember, we must
take responsibility.

The only reason we get irritated by trifles, according to
Seneca, is because we didn't expect them. "This is due to
excessive self-love. We decide that we ought not to be

harmed even by our enemies; each one in his heart has the king's point of view, and is willing to use license, but unwilling to suffer from it."

We're spoiled and kick and scream like a child when the world doesn't bend to our king's point of view. We only have in mind what we think the world owes us, and forget being grateful for what we're lucky to have.

Our overoptimistic expectations and desires are the main reasons for our anger and frustration. Therefore, we must bring them more in line with reality, and we won't feel like let down by the world. As seen before, if we only desire what's within our control, then we can never be frustrated regardless of the circumstances.

As aspiring Stoics, we should try to see the world as it really is, rather than demanding that it fits our expectations. We must remind ourselves what the world is like, what we can expect to encounter in it, and what lies within our own control. The wise person, says Seneca, "will ensure that none of what happens will come unexpectedly."

"What is quite unlooked for is more crushing in its effect, and unexpectedness adds to the weight of a disaster. The fact that it was unforeseen has never failed to intensify a person's grief. This is a reason for ensuring that nothing ever takes us by surprise. We should project our thoughts ahead of us at every turn and have in mind every possible eventuality instead of only the usual course of events."

As encountered earlier, devastation depends on how unlikely we considered an event in the first place.

That's why it's so important to keep our expectations in check by regularly engaging in negative visualization. If we imagine the worst, we won't have to deal with unmet expectations and can drastically reduce the negative emotions we experience.

Let's mentally rehearse the worst that could happen and see how a situation can unfold contrary to our hopes and expectations—and we'll be at peace with whatever happens.

We shouldn't be surprised by anything, especially not by things that happen on a regular basis.

"Remember," says Marcus Aurelius, "you shouldn't be surprised that a fig tree produces figs, nor the world what it produces. A good doctor isn't surprised when his patients have fevers, or a helmsman when the wind blows against him."

Practice 27

Pain and Provocation: Great Opportunities for Virtue

"For every challenge, remember the resources you have
within you to cope with it. Provoked by the sight of a
handsome man or a beautiful woman, you will discover
within you the contrary power of self-restraint. Faced with
pain, you will discover the power of endurance. If you are
insulted, you will discover patience. In time, you will grow to
be confident that there is not a single impression that you will
not have the moral means to tolerate."

– EPICTETUS

"What stands in the way becomes the way," as seen earlier
(Practice 3).

We can turn seeming adversity into an advantage by
using it as practice. As warrior-philosophers, we use these
situations to practice being the best we can be.

While other people see adversity as bad, as something
preventing them from achieving their goals, we recognize the

opportunity for growth and flip it around—we see opportunity where they see evil.

"Disease is an impediment to the body, but not to the will, unless the will itself chooses," explains Epictetus. "Lameness is an impediment to the leg, but not to the will."

Epictetus had a lame leg, and he decided to look at it as an impediment to the leg, not the mind. Pain and sickness, too, are to the body, not the mind. We must not allow to be taken over by self-pity. Such a self-indulgent response will only increase our suffering.

Instead, we must remember that pain can be an opportunity to test and improve our virtue. We can practice patience and endurance—two noble strengths.

Marcus agrees, "Who is there to prevent you from being good and sincere?" We have the inborn power to choose our actions and craft our character. "So display those virtues which are wholly in your own power—integrity, dignity, hard work, self-denial, contentment, frugality, kindness, independence, simplicity, discretion, magnanimity."

We can display so many great qualities without any excuse. The only thing that can hold us back is ourselves, because the mind is always available to us.

Just like nature can take every obstacle and turn it to its purposes, says Marcus, "so, too, a rational being can turn each setback into raw material and use it to achieve its goal."

We should start with small things, says Epictetus. If we have a headache, we can practice not to curse. If it's abusive words, we can practice patience. And he underlines that if we complain, we must make sure not to complain with our whole being.

Let's remind ourselves that every minor accident that happens to us presents an opportunity to practice virtuous behavior. Every headache is a chance not to curse. Every attractive person is a chance for self-restraint. Every annoying person is a chance for patience, kindness, and forgiveness. Every challenging situation is a chance for perseverance and hard-work.

Practice 28

The Equanimity Game

"When force of circumstance upsets your equanimity, lose no time in recovering your self-control, and do not remain out of tune longer than you can help. Habitual recurrence to the harmony will increase your mastery of it."
– MARCUS AURELIUS

We all get caught off guard from time to time. Not just by major events, but also by minor, often unexpected, occurrences. The train doesn't arrive on time, your bike gets stolen, your friend cancels the date at last minute.

Such insignificant situations can knock us out in weak moments. We lose balance and become irritable and grouchy. It's totally ok to get thrown out of balance sometimes, it happens to the best of us. What matters is to get back on track as soon as possible.

Don't be knocked out any longer than necessary. Get a hold on yourself and get back up! Return to balance.

Modern philosopher Brian Johnson calls this the "equanimity game." The rules are simple: (1) notice when you're off-balance, for example, when you start to lose your patience with the traffic, your spouse, or a colleague, then (2) see how fast you can catch yourself and correct yourself—bringing yourself back to equanimity.

He says *equanimity* is one of the greatest words ever. From the Latin: *aequus* (even) and *animus* (mind), the word means "balanced mind."

So we should catch ourselves whenever we get thrown off-balance by some event, and then get back to a balanced mind as quickly as possible. Setbacks happen, we won't always be our best. The wise person knows this and their main goal is to recover as quickly as possible. Like a punching ball that rebounds whenever you hit it.

We want to live with areté and express our highest self at all times. So when we catch ourselves lagging behind, let's try to recover and get back on track. We can collect turn-arounds in this game. And we'll get better the more often we catch ourselves and get back in balance.

"Habitual recurrence to the harmony will increase your mastery of it," as Marcus teaches us.

Always remember: Obstacles and challenging situations make us stronger, they're an opportunity for growth. We want to be warriors of the mind who don't retreat but try to be fully present in the face of life's challenges—well aware that these challenges will make us stronger.

Earlier, we said that a fire uses obstacles as fuel. They only make the fire stronger. Now, let's look at another fire metaphor: The wind fuels a fire and extinguishes a candle. The wind is the obstacle; it extinguishes you if your commitment and perseverance are weak, but it fuels you when you accept the challenge and don't give up with the first difficulties.

If you blow at a candle, it extinguishes. If you blow into a campfire, it might seem to extinguish at first but it comes back stronger. You want to be the fire that always comes back stronger.

So whenever life hits you, notice what knocks you down, and then see how long it takes you to get back up. Observe yourself and find out what helps you find your balance. You can play that game all day, every day.

What helps me most are the Stoic ideas to focus on what you control, to accept reality as it is, and to take responsibility for my life as it's always within my power to choose to respond with virtue.

Practice 29

The Anti-Puppet Mindset

"If a person gave away your body to some passersby, you'd
be furious. Yet you hand over your mind to anyone who
comes along, so they may abuse you, leaving it disturbed and
troubled—have you no shame in that?"

– EPICTETUS

We get jerked around by external things and unquestioned
impulses all the time. Like puppets, we let someone else pull
the strings and dance to their liking.

The ambiguous remark of a colleague, the boyfriend who
didn't call, or the comment of a stranger—we get spun
around by things beyond our control. We let others push our
buttons.

Even worse, it's not just other people, we also let the
weather, social media, news, and sports results pull our
strings. We dance to sunshine and stomp to rain. We cheer
the goal of our favorite team, and bemoan the late equalizer.

This is madness. The mind is our own. Not our body, our
possessions, our friends, but only our mind. But we're

unaware and oops, it's in the hand of the weatherman or the ref.

"Understand at last that you have something in you more powerful and divine than what causes the bodily passions and pulls you like a mere puppet."

What Marcus means is our mind. We can decide what external events mean to us. We don't have to get jerked around by what happens around us. We can actually remain calm without getting hurt and irritated.

Just cut the strings that pull your mind. Take back what's meant to be yours. Stop the madness. Don't get pulled by what's not under your control.

Yes, says Marcus, others can impede our actions, but they can't impede our intentions and our attitudes. Our mind is adaptable. If things seem to turn against us, we can adapt and see the opportunity for growth. We can convert obstacles into opportunities.

Instead of getting jerked around by what happens in the uncontrollable world outside, we should be guided by deep values. No matter what happens, we stick to our values of tranquility, patience, kindness, acceptance, justice, grit, and self-discipline.

Our values and mindfulness of the present moment prevent us from being puppets. These things won't come automatically but require hard work. As aspiring Stoics, we choose to work hard and become our own masters rather than getting jerked around by every inconvenience.

"Frame your thoughts like this—you are an old person, you won't let yourself be enslaved by this any longer, no longer pulled like a puppet by every impulse, and you'll stop complaining about your present fortune or dreading the future."

Marcus sets a great frame here. Let's use this one: We're a mature human being and won't be enslaved by outside events and other people any longer. We won't be pulled like a puppet by every impulse. We won't complain about the present moment or dread the future.

It's time to take back control.

Let's protect our peace of mind.

"The first thing to do—don't get worked up." Marcus reminds himself to stay calm. Once you have a hold on yourself, consider the task at hand for what it is, while keeping your values in mind. Then take appropriate action with kindness, modesty, and sincerity.

First, don't get upset. Second, do the right thing. That's it.

If we bring awareness into the situation, this is always available to us. We try not to get upset at first. And then look at it objectively while keeping our values in mind. And act accordingly.

This process requires us to notice our impulses, impressions, and judgments so that we can step back from them rather than allowing them to sweep us away. We must avoid rashness in our reactions. That's all.

Avoid rashness, stay calm, and you won't get jerked around like a puppet.

Practice 30

Life Is Supposed to Be Challenging

"Difficulties show a person's character. So when a challenge
confronts you, remember that God is matching you with a
younger sparring partner, as would a physical trainer. Why?
Becoming an Olympian takes sweat! I think no one has a
better challenge than yours, if only you would use it like an
athlete would that younger sparring partner."

– EPICTETUS

We're quick to complain about a situation.

But who said it's going to be fair? Who said life should
be easy?

No one. That's what we're here for! We're meant for this.
It's how we get better. It's how we learn to endure and
persevere. It's how we grow into a mature human being.

"What would have become of Hercules, do you think, if
there had been no lion, hydra, stag or boar—and no savage
criminals to rid the world of? What would he have done in
the absence of such challenges?"

This Hercules example Epictetus makes is worth repeating. He goes on: "Obviously he would have just rolled over in bed and gone back to sleep. So by snoring his life away in luxury and comfort he never would have developed into the mighty Hercules. And even if he had, what good would it have done him? What would have been the use of those arms, that physique, and that noble soul, without crises or conditions to stir him into action?"

Don't wish for life to be hard, but neither wish for it to be easier when it gets tough. Rather wish for the strength to deal with it. It's an opportunity for growth. It's the younger sparring partner who's challenging you. He's just testing you.

The question is: What do you do with the challenge? Are you the one who accepts it and is ready to tackle it head-on? Or are you the one who throws in the towel after the first hook to the chin?

This is what we're here for, say the Stoics. Life is supposed to be hard. It's even unfortunate if you don't have to face these challenges. Hear out Seneca: "I judge you unfortunate because you have never lived through misfortune. You have passed through life without an opponent—no one can ever know what you are capable of, not even you."

That's why the Stoics were engaged in life. They knew that's where we grow, not in the ivory towers.

Next time you're facing a tough situation, accept it as a chance for growth. Don't worry about it. You can only grow. Maybe it's a formative experience you'll be grateful for later.

The question is not *if* life will throw some punches at you, but *when*. And how you'll respond to it.

Will you respond in a growth-oriented and positive way—ready to tackle it? Or will you respond like a victim—

complaining and throwing in the towel at the first indication of difficulty?

Do you see it as a chance to learn and get stronger? Or do you get frustrated and start crying?

So when it gets tough, remind yourself it's what you're here for. It'll make you stronger.

Practice 31

What's so Troublesome
Here and Now?

"Do not let the panorama of your life oppress you, do not
dwell on all the various troubles which may have occurred in
the past or may occur in the future. Just ask yourself in each
instance of the present: 'What is there in this work
which I cannot endure or support?'"
– MARCUS AURELIUS

An important part of Stoicism is developing moment-to-
moment awareness that allows you to take a step back, look
at the situation objectively, analyze your impressions, and
proceed with what's constructive.

In a hectic moment, it's easy to lose focus on the task at
hand and get lost in the vastness of our lives. We look far in
the uncertain future and back in the certain but gone past. No
wonder we get overwhelmed.

Let's not forget that the past and the future are not under
our control. They are indifferent to the Stoics. The present
moment is all anyone possesses, says Marcus. But "no one

can lose either the past or the future, for how can someone be deprived of what's not theirs?"

The past is unchangeably gone. The future can only be influenced by the actions we take here and now. That's why the Stoics say we must be mindful in the present moment and focus on what's real and graspable.

The whole power we have comes down to this very moment. Right now, we can control the choices we make. You choose to read this book now, what I chose to write right now (for me).

Our voluntary thoughts and actions are the only things under our control. Only in this very moment.

If we want to express our highest self in every moment, then we *need* to be aware of our actions in the present moment. This mindfulness is a prerequisite for the practicing Stoic.

The struggle is this: We get carried away by our thoughts about the past or future. And all the while lose touch with the here and now. This is the main reason why we get overwhelmed. Unlike animals, we worry about what's long gone or yet to come, both beyond our control. Hear out Seneca: "Wild beasts run away from dangers when they see them. Once they have escaped, they are free of anxiety. But we are tormented by both the future and the past."

The present alone, he says, cannot make you miserable.

That's why we should try to catch ourselves when we're overwhelmed, and ask: "Right here, right now, what's the task at hand and why does it seem unbearable?"

If you're able to focus on the present moment, and look at it in an isolated way, then these challenging moments will suddenly become easier to endure and deal with. It'll be easier to accept them as they are, and focus on what you can do right now to improve your situation, to make the best out of it.

One tiny step at a time.

The better you become at retrieving your focus into the present moment, the more mindful you'll become of your moment to moment actions, and the closer you'll get to express your highest self.

Marcus Aurelius says that all you'll ever need is:

- **Certainty of judgment in the present moment:** What does the situation look like objectively?
- **Acceptance of external events in the present moment:** Accept and be content with what's out of control.
- **Action for the common good in the present moment:** What's the best action I can take right now?

If that's all you take away from Stoic philosophy, and if you bring enough mindfulness into your daily life, then you'll benefit greatly!

As aspiring Stoics, we should try to focus on the present moment, and not get distracted by the past or future. That's the only way we can challenge our impressions and look at the situation objectively, accept what's not under our control with equanimity, and choose to align our actions with our deepest values such as wisdom, justice, courage, and self-discipline.

This will suffice.

Practice 32

Count Your Blessings

"Don't set your mind on things you don't possess as if they were yours, but count the blessings you actually possess and think how much you would desire them if they weren't already yours. But watch yourself, that you don't value these things to the point of being troubled if you should lose them."

– MARCUS AURELIUS

In times of struggles, it can be helpful to remember what we have. Because we forget how good we actually have it, and how kind life has been with us in the past.

Don't forget to be thankful for what you have—even in the face of adversity.

Marcus reminds us here of three things:

- Material things are not important, don't gather and hoard that stuff.
- Be grateful for all you have.
- Be careful not to get attached to those things.

Who cares what others have? You can decide for yourself what's truly important and what isn't. Focus on yourself. Recognize how life has been generous with you. You don't need more and more stuff. You need less. And you'll be freer.

The more you have, the more you can lose. Be grateful for what you have. Appreciate those things. And find ways to take advantage of what you already have.

Here's a divine law Epictetus generously shares with us: "And what is the divine law? To keep a man's own, not to claim that which belongs to others, but to use what is given, and when it is not given, not to desire it; and when a thing is taken away, to give it up readily and immediately, and to be thankful for the time that a man has had the use of it."

Desire not what you don't have, but appreciate what you do have. Always be ready to give back what you've been given, and be thankful for the time it was yours to use.

What a simple law. Let's tattoo that into our minds.

Seneca agrees: "The greatest blessings of mankind are within us . . . A wise man is content with his lot, whatever it may be, without wishing for what he has not."

Let's keep such an attitude of gratitude at all times. For everything we have, and for everything that comes our way.

Make sure to be grateful on a regular basis. The easiest way to do that is to write down a few specific things you're grateful for each day. Add that to your morning routine when you say Marcus' words: "When you arise in the morning, think of what a precious privilege it is to be alive—to breathe, to think, to enjoy, to love."

Remember not to cling to those things. They're only borrowed from nature and can be taken away at a snap.

Practice 33

Other-ize

"We can familiarize ourselves with the will of nature by
calling to mind our common experiences. When a friend
breaks a glass, we are quick to say, 'Oh, bad luck.' It's only
reasonable, then, that when a glass of your own breaks, you
accept it in the same patient spirit . . . We would do better to
remember how we react when a similar loss afflicts others."

– EPICTETUS

How differently we look at the same event when it happens
to us rather than to other people.

When your colleague breaks a cup, you take it easy and
might make a comment such as the German proverb, "Shards
bring good fortune," or "Shit happens, let me help you clean
it up."

But when it happens to us, we're quick to judge ourselves
as clumsy or incapable. Naturally, it's far easier to remain
calm and maintain equanimity when misfortunes happen to
others rather than to ourselves.

Wouldn't it be smarter to react similarly when something affects us? I mean, we're not special. So why would we make a mountain out of a molehill when something affects us, but tick it off with a smile when it happens to others?

This doesn't make sense. The universe doesn't treat us any differently than others, it's not after us. Things just happen, sometimes to us, sometimes to others. Things happen to us in the normal order of things. Get comfort in that.

Next time something inconveniently happens to you, imagine it happened to someone else. Ask yourself how you'd react when the same happened to your colleague Sharon. If it's not terrible when it happens to Sharon, then it's not terrible when it happens to you.

This will make you aware of the relative insignificance of the "bad" things that happen to all of us and will therefore prevent you from disrupting your tranquility.

Epictetus takes it a step further: "Moving on to graver things: when somebody's wife or child dies, to a man we all routinely say, 'Well, that's part of life.' But if one of our own family is involved, then right away it's 'Poor, poor me!'"

With a broken cup, this is much easier than with a broken heart. Yet it's the same thing. Why is it not too bad when Sharon loses her husband, but it's the worst that could happen when it's your husband?

Look, we can't just tick off the death of a loved one like the death of a cup. But thinking about our reaction if it happened to someone else might be helpful nonetheless. It brings in some perspective and reminds us what happens to us happens to others as well.

Similarly, it can help you become more empathic and understanding to others when you imagine that what happened to them happened to you. We're sometimes quick to judge someone as overreacting and dismiss their feelings, but when the same happens to us, we'd be the same. Or even worse.

So, when some inconvenience happens to you, think about the reaction you'd show if it happened to someone else. This will help you maintain your balanced mind.

Also, before you judge someone's reaction to a misfortune, think about your own reaction to the same misfortune. This will help you be more understanding toward others.

Practice 34

Take the Bird's-Eye View

"How beautifully Plato put it. Whenever you want to talk about people, it's best to take a bird's-eye view and see everything all at once—of gatherings, armies, farms, weddings and divorces, births and deaths, noisy courtrooms or silent places, every foreign people, holidays, memorials, markets—all blended together and arranged in a pairing of opposites."

– MARCUS AURELIUS

What a great exercise. Imagine you leave your body and float up in the sky. Higher and higher. You see yourself, your house, your neighborhood, other people, your town with its lake and river, until your body seems like a tiny seed, and further you go to see your country, the ocean, and even the whole planet.

This exercise helps you recognize yourself as a part of the whole. You see all human things from far above, like a bird first, and then like an astronaut.

"You can rid yourself of many useless things among those that disturb you," Marcus observes, "for they lie entirely in your imagination." Many problems can be solved with this perspective from far above. Human affairs and your own misfortunes seem trivial from this perspective.

"And by contemplating the eternity of time, and observing the rapid change of every part of everything, how short is the time from birth to dissolution, and the illimitable time before birth as well as the equally boundless time after dissolution."

Not only do our problems seem insignificant and dissolve quickly, but we also get reminded of the impermanence of things. We're not only very small, but also very ephemeral. He says it perfectly: "Continually picture to yourself time and space as a whole, and every individual thing, in terms of space a tiny seed, in terms of time the mere turn of a screw."

Next time you're troubled, try taking a bird's-eye perspective.

We often get caught up in our minds. So we screw up and imagine it to be a big deal. We're lost in thought and don't recognize its banality. We focus on the problem at hand and it seems like the most important thing on earth. Like a massive problem.

That's when you want to take this view from far above. Your massive problem suddenly gets utterly insignificant compared to the vastness of the universe. This helps you put things in perspective, recognize the bigger picture, and stay indifferent to external things others mistakenly value—like wealth, looks, or social status.

Practice 35

It's the Same Old Things

> "Everything that happens is as simple and familiar as
> the rose in spring, the fruit in summer: disease, death,
> blasphemy, conspiracy . . . everything that makes
> stupid people happy or angry."
> – MARCUS AURELIUS

"One generation passeth away, and another generation cometh: but the earth abideth forever." Although this could be from Marcus Aurelius, it's actually from the Bible.

Things have always been the same. Human beings have been doing what they do. Certain attitudes and practices have come and gone, but people and lives have always been the same—marrying, raising children, falling ill, dying, fighting, crying, laughing, feasting, pretending, grumbling, falling in love, lusting, and philosophizing.

Nothing new. The things are the same as ten generations ago, and will be the same in future generations. Seneca, Epictetus, and Marcus Aurelius had the same struggles as we're having two thousand years later, that's why their texts are still so relevant today. Marcus reminds us that everything keeps recurring. "Evil: the same old thing. No matter what happens, keep this in mind: It's the same old thing, from one end of the world to the other. It fills the history books, ancient and modern, and the cities, and the houses too. Nothing new at all."

It's easy to believe that what's happening now is special. But as strong people, we must resist this notion, and be aware that with a few exceptions, things are the same as they've always been and always will be. The same old things.

We're just like the people who came before us. We're just brief stopovers until other people just like us will come when we're gone. The earth abides forever, but we will come and go.

Before you take things too seriously, remind yourself that things that happen to you are not special. Hundreds have experienced it before you, and hundreds more will once you're gone.

Sorry to tell you, but you're not so special. What happens to you is not so special. How you behave is not so special.

This might help you put things in perspective. And not take everything so seriously. And not take yourself too seriously. It's the same old things.

Also, this is another reason why we shouldn't be surprised at trifles—those things happen again and again, we might want to be aware of that. Things break, people die, games get lost, people fail—as the rose in spring and the fruits in summer—things will always recur.

Practice 36

Meat Is Dead Animal:
Observe Objectively

"When we have meat before us and such eatables, we receive
the impression that this is the dead body of a fish, and this is
the dead body of a bird or of a pig; and again, that this
Falernian [wine] is only a little grape juice, and this purple
robe some sheep's wool dyed with the blood of a shellfish;
or, in the matter of sexual intercourse, that it is merely an
internal attrition and the spasmodic expulsion of semen: such
then are these impressions, and they reach the things
themselves and penetrate them, and so we see
the things as they truly are."
– MARCUS AURELIUS

The Stoics advise to look at an object or a situation as
objectively as possible. Stick to the facts and describe an
event as value-free and as close to reality as possible.

That's classic Stoic thinking: An event itself is objective.
Only we give it meaning by our judgments about it.

As seen above, Marcus reminds himself to look at the basic constituents of things. He wants to make sure he doesn't attribute too much importance to external things.

(As a side note: The part about sexual intercourse is not meant to be prudish—after all, Marcus had 13 children—but rather as a check against lust for lust's sake.)

We should look at things as they are, "lay them bare and look at their worthlessness and strip them of all the words by which they are exalted."

We should see an event for what it is, analyze it, "turn it inside out and see what it is like, what it becomes in age, sickness, death."

Marcus turns things inside out and looks at them carefully. He speaks of his emperor's robes as "some sheep's wool dyed with the blood of a shellfish." Although it might be expensive, it's just some sheep's wool dyed with blood of foul-smelling *murex* shellfish extracts. If you paid attention, you might remember that this dye was the cargo Zeno lost in his shipwreck many years before he founded Stoicism.

Things might actually be precious, but if looked at objectively, they become quite worthless.

Marcus advises to live through life in the best way we can. The power to do so is found in a person's soul, if she can be indifferent to external things. And she will be indifferent if she "looks at these things both as a whole and analyzed into their parts, and remembers that none of them imposes a judgment of itself or forces itself on us."

Basically, looking at things objectively, as they really are, will help express the highest version of ourselves. We'll recognize their utter insignificance and remember that it's only our value judgments that give them value and meaning.

In Stoic philosophy, we look at things from every angle and get to understand situations better. Oftentimes, the objective representation of events helps us see clearly and hinders us from giving them too much meaning.

So, when you're challenged in life, when you're stuck, try to look at your situation objectively. Turn it inside out, strip it naked, and explain it in simple terms. As real as possible. What does it look like? What parts does it consist of? How long will it last?

Practice 37

Avoid Rashness:
Test Your Impressions (!)

"So make a practice at once of saying to every strong impression: 'An impression is all you are, not the source of the impression.' Then test and assess it with your criteria, but one primarily: ask, 'Is this something that is, or is not, in my control?' And if it's not one of the things that you control, be ready with the reaction, 'Then it's none of my concern.'"

– EPICTETUS

We're naturally evolved to approach what feels good, and avoid what feels bad. That's our survival instinct. And it massively influences our behavior in everyday life.

It's the main reason why we procrastinate. And it's the main reason why we swear at other drivers while driving. Some stimulus triggers an impression and we act upon it. In most cases, this happens automatically:

- A driver cuts us off and we yell at him.
- Grandma serves us cookies and we eat them.
- Our brother is watching TV, so we sit down and watch with him.

The problem with that? Our senses are wrong all the time. Our emotional impressions are counterproductive in today's world. If we only approach what feels good, we end up wasting our lives binge-watching Netflix, binge-eating M&Ms, and binge-drinking Goon!

The point is, what *feels* right is often not the right thing to do.

Remember, as aspiring Stoics, we want to stay at the steering wheel at all times so we can deliberately choose our best actions. This is why it's crucial we don't react impulsively to impressions, but take a moment before we react, and it'll be much easier to maintain control.

We must avoid rashness in our actions. As Epictetus says: "Be not swept off your feet by the vividness of the impression, but say: 'Wait for me a little, impression: allow me to see who you are, and what you are an impression of; allow me to put you to the test.'"

Let's put our impressions to the test. Is this really so bad? What happened exactly? Do I really want to go down that path? Why do I feel such a strong urge within me? What do I know about this person?

If you're able to pause and ask such questions, you'll be less likely to get carried away by the impressions and make a rash move. It's all about withholding automatic reactions. Refuse to accept your impulsive impression. Test it first.

Now this isn't easy. If we want to put our impressions to the test, if we want to step back and look at them as mere hypotheses, then we must be able to spot them in the first place. This requires self-awareness.

So it's really two steps: First, spot our impressions and make sure we don't get carried away immediately. Second, examine the impressions and calmly decide what to do next.

The ability to postpone our reactions to passionate impressions by saying, "Wait for me a little, impression" is the basis of living with areté. It's the only way we can abstain from doing what feels good and do the things that don't.

If you're able to avoid rashness in your actions and have the necessary self-discipline, then you become the person who's able to say no to the things others can't resist, and able to do the things others dread doing.

You see, testing your impressions is really a core quality of every aspiring Stoic. As you keep doing that, you will also realize that it's not the event itself but your reaction to it that upsets or delights you. If you choose not to react at all to minor inconveniences, you simply won't care anymore. As if nothing happened.

If we simply gain time and wait before we react, then we'll be able to resist our impulses to react instinctively and immediately. These impulsive reactions are not helpful in most cases.

This is all about avoiding rash emotional reactions. And then testing primarily whether there's something we can do about it or not. Let's not concern ourselves with what's beyond our control—precisely because there's nothing we can do about it.

Only our reaction is within our control. So let's choose our smartest (non-)reaction, and move on. Let's hear Epictetus' strategy to deal with pleasurable impressions: "Whenever you get an impression of some pleasure, as with any impression, guard yourself from being carried away by it, let it await your action, give yourself a pause. After that, bring to mind both times, first when you have enjoyed the pleasure and later when you will regret it and hate yourself. Then compare to those the joy and satisfaction you'd feel for abstaining it altogether."

Take-away: Before you react, say: "Wait for me a little, impression . . . allow me to put you to the test."

Practice 38

Do Good, Be Good

"Don't behave as if you are destined to live forever. What's

fated hangs over you. As long as you live and

while you can, become good now."

– MARCUS AURELIUS

What are you reading this book for?

You won't get a badge of honor or some other award for learning about Stoicism. Nobody cares what books you read or what you know about ancient philosophy.

And you don't care either because you read it for yourself. Because you want to be the best you can be. Because you want to be able to deal effectively with life's challenges. Because you want to live a happy and smoothly flowing life.

And that's what it's all about. "For philosophy doesn't consist in outward display," Musonius Rufus reminds us, "but in taking heed to what is needed and being mindful of it."

It's who you are and what you do that matters. It's human excellence that makes a human being beautiful, says

Epictetus. If you develop qualities such as justice, tranquility, courage, self-discipline, kindness, or patience you will become beautiful.

Nobody can cheat themselves to true beauty.

Good and bad lie in our choices. It's what we choose to do with the given cards that matters. If you try to be good, if you try your best, the outcome doesn't matter.

You can get good from yourself. "The fortunate person is the one who gives themselves good fortune," says Marcus. "And good fortunes are a well-tuned soul, good impulses and good actions."

Joy comes from your choices, from your deliberately chosen actions. Well-intentioned actions will bring peace of mind. It's your best chance for happiness.

Do good because it's the right thing to do. Don't look for anything in return. Do it for yourself. So you can be the person you want to be.

Don't be the guy who shouts from the rooftops when done a just act. "Simply move on to the next deed just like the vine produces another bunch of grapes in the right season." Marcus reminds us to do good for its own sake.

It's our nature. It's our job.

It's childish behavior to tell what good you've done. As a child, when I did something that benefitted our whole family, I made sure everybody knew what I've done. But my mom? My dad? They did those exact things day in, day out without anyone noticing. We kids took everything for granted. Mostly thankless.

As we ripen, we understand that doing the right thing and helping others is simply what we have to do. It's our duty as smart, responsible, and mature human beings. Nothing else.

It's just what leaders do—not for the thanks, recognition, or the badge of honor.

"Do now what nature demands of you. Get right to it if that's in your power. Don't look around to see if people will know about it."

As the Roman Emperor, Marcus certainly had more power than we have, and his actions had a bigger impact than yours and mine. Yet, even the most powerful man on earth at that time reminded himself to "be satisfied with even the smallest step forward and regard the outcome as a small thing."

Let's take a small step forward whenever possible. What comes from it? It doesn't matter.

"What is your profession? Being a good man."

That's the simplest job description there is. Which doesn't mean it's easy. But if we make it our goal to be good, then I'm positive we can get there. One good deed at a time.

Chapter 8

Situational Practices

How to Handle Yourself When Other
People Challenge You?

The most difficult and frequent challenges we face in everyday life are other people.

Every day, there's at least one annoying person who tries to push your buttons. That reckless driver, the barefaced secretary, the mindless skater body, or the nagging little brother.

Now we can't get rid of these people. We have a life. We work with people. We have family and friends. And most importantly, we have a social duty. Stoic philosophy demands to help others and to be concerned with the wellbeing of all mankind.

Remember, we should treat other people as relatives as we're all citizens of the same world. We must contribute some service to the community. We're social because we cannot exist without one another. And doing good to others benefits ourselves first and foremost.

As Marcus says, fulfilling our social duties will give you the best chance at living a good life.

But other people can be so nerve-wracking:

- People lie to your face
- People insult you
- People hurt your feelings
- People cheat you
- People steal from you
- People annoy you

So how can we preserve our tranquility while fulfilling our social duties and interacting with other people? That's what the following practices and strategies are all about.

Practice 39

We Are All Limbs of the Same Body

"I, then, can neither be harmed by these people, nor become angry with one who is akin to me, nor can I hate him, for we have come into being to work together, like feet, hands, eyelids, or the two rows of teeth in our upper and lower jaws. To work against one another is therefore contrary to nature; and to be angry with another person and turn away from him is surely to work against him."

– MARCUS AURELIUS

You and me, we're relatives. I am your brother. You are my brother or sister. We're made for cooperation.

"Constantly think of the universe as a single living being," says Marcus. We must recognize ourselves as a limb of a larger body and work together: "Since you yourself are one of the parts that serve to perfect a social system, let your every action contribute to the perfecting of social life."

Let your actions contribute to the wellbeing of mankind. You are a limb of the whole. We must work together. Seneca agrees by saying that Mother Nature gave birth to us as relatives. And she instilled in us a mutual love.

We stem from the same source. "Our fellowship is very similar to an arch of stones, which would fall apart, if they did not reciprocally support each other." We must support each other or the whole will fall apart. We're all interconnected and depending on one another.

Working for each other is necessary if we want to live the best life possible. That means for you as a limb of the whole. Help others. Direct your actions for the common welfare. That's the only way you'll have a good life.

If we fail to recognize this interconnectedness, and if we fail to direct our actions to these social ends, then we tear our lives apart, says Marcus. This will create a separation and disharmony. And we won't be able to live good lives.

Remember that we humans are created for one another. We're born to work together the way our hands and eyelids do. Our actions should serve mankind with harmony as the goal.

Let's do good to others and treat them as brothers and sisters, with patience, kindness, forgiveness, and generosity. This is the only way to the good life.

Remember Marcus' words: "What brings no benefit to the hive brings none to the bee."

Practice 40

Nobody Errs on Purpose

"When a man assents, then, to what is false, know that he had
no wish to assent to the false: 'for no soul is robbed of the
truth with its own consent,' as Plato says,
but the false seemed to him true."

– EPICTETUS

People do what seems right to them. If they do wrong, it's
because that's what seems true to them.

Therefore, we should not blame people, even if they treat
us rudely and unfairly. They don't do those things on
purpose. As Socrates said: "Nobody does wrong willingly."

Jesus said something very similar after he was forced to
bear his own cross, and got beaten, flogged, and insulted.
Despite the unpleasantness of the situation, Jesus looked up
to the sky and said, "Father, forgive them, for they don't
know what they are doing."

The Stoics believe people act as they think is the best way
for them to act. If people lie, it's because they think this will
benefit them. If people steal, they think it's the best thing to

do. If people are mean, they somehow have the impression that's how they get the most out of the situation.

They lack certain wisdom. They don't know what's right and what's wrong. And even if they know what they're doing might be wrong, they're still mistaken and think it'll be to their advantage.

The point is, they don't do wrong on purpose. They just don't understand any better.

We must be patient with these people. "Some people are sharp and others dull," Musonius reminds us, and goes on: "Some are raised in a better environment, others in worse, the latter, having inferior habits and nurture, will require more by way of proof and careful instruction to master these teachings and to be formed by them—in the same way that bodies in a bad state must be given great deal of care when perfect health is ought."

Let's not forget that we're privileged. Not everybody had the same upbringing as we had. Not all have them same genes, education, and early exposure. These things highly influence a person, and it's not something we can control.

Just like a body in bad shape needs more time to heal than one in good shape, a person who lacks a lot of wisdom needs longer to catch up and understand than a person who had the wisest parents and best schooling.

It makes no sense to be angry with these people. It's not their fault. A much better way to deal with them is to lead by example. Instead of reacting angrily, react in a kind and understanding way. Instead of judging them, try to help and support them.

Whenever you come across a situation with people who seem to act wrongly, it's an opportunity for growth. Because you can practice the virtues of self-control, forgiveness, kindness, and patience.

Marcus says it's important to keep this in mind: "As Plato said, every soul is deprived of truth against its will. The same holds true for justice, self-control, goodwill to others, and every similar virtue. It's essential to constantly keep this in your mind, for it will make you more gentle to all."

Practice 41

Find Your Own Faults

"Whenever you take offense at someone's wrongdoing,
immediately turn to your own similar failings, such as seeing
money as good, or pleasure, or a little fame—whatever form
it takes. By thinking on this, you'll quickly forget your anger,
considering also what compels them—for what else could
they do? Or, if you are able, remove their compulsion."

– MARCUS AURELIUS

To err is human.

We all make mistakes. But we forget. And get angry
when others make the same mistakes we made not long ago.

As you know by now, people don't err on purpose. Just
bring to mind all the times you did wrong without malice or
intention. The time you did not speak the exact truth. The
time you acted on bad information. The time you were
shockingly rude because of your lovesickness. The time you
didn't listen, misunderstood, and thus did the exact opposite.

Don't write people off for erring. We all have bad
moments.

"When you are offended at any man's fault," Epictetus tells us, "turn to yourself and study your own failings. Then you will forget your anger."

Often, when we judge others for their misbehavior, we're actually not better at all. We just like to *think* we are.

Study your own failings. There are plenty of them. We're just generous with our own faults and wave them through freely. Because we think to know that *actually* we don't do this, we only mean good, and in *reality* we're better and don't allow such behavior. It's an exception this time.

We let us slip under the radar because our brain rationalizes our faults beautifully. But as soon as we detect others doing the same, the alarm goes off immediately, and we point a finger at them and are quick to render an all but mild judgment.

Let's not get carried away by our initial impression that the other is a jerk, but let's bring to mind that we've been there before. We've been that exact jerk before. And we judged us mildly at most.

And even if you become more and more aware of your faults, correct them, and actually don't make the same mistakes anymore, always remain calm and understanding toward others. Remember two things: First, they don't err on purpose. Second, you've made many mistakes up to now. And still counting.

There's actually a second part to the opening proverb: To err is human; to forgive, divine.

Practice 42

Forgive and Love Those Who Stumble

"Whenever you meet someone, say to yourself from the outset, 'What are his assumptions concerning what is fundamentally good and bad in life?' When someone acts like your enemy, insults or opposes you, remember that he was only doing what seemed to him the right thing, he didn't know any better, and tell yourself: 'It seemed so to him.'"

– EPICTETUS

Stoicism calls for forgiveness.

The Stoics remind themselves of the ignorance of the wrongdoers. They don't do wrong on purpose, but what they do seems to be the right thing in their situations.

It's our special privilege says Marcus, "to love even those who stumble." He reminds himself of four things: (1) that the stumbling people are relatives, (2) they do wrong involuntarily, (3) we will all be dead soon anyway, and (4) we can only be harmed if we choose so.

Therefore, it's within our power (and duty) to love even those who stumble. Seneca likewise says, "Bestow pardon for many things; seek pardon for none."

He's well aware that others do what seems true to them and, therefore, he freely pardons them. And at the same time he knows that if they don't pardon him, it's because it doesn't seem necessary to them.

Be forgiving, even if others aren't. You lead by example, knowing that they don't see what you see.

In a sense, the Stoics view stumbling people as misguided and lacking in wisdom, more like children than malicious people. They fail to recognize that what they're doing isn't even in their own best interest. They are blind to see. It's like an illness.

They don't see what they're doing. And because they're ill, it's not like they had a choice in that matter. So who are we to blame them? Let's not resent what they do, because that's like resenting their illness.

The only appropriate response is compassion and forgiveness.

Marcus makes a neat comparison: He says wishing for the unknowing man not to do wrong is like wishing for a fig tree not to produce figs, babies not to cry, and horses not to neigh. These are inevitable things. They just happen by nature.

Don't wish for people not to do wrong, rather wish for the strength to be tolerant and forgiving.

Imagine how much more forgiving you'd be if you could see other people's missteps as inevitable, natural, or stemming from an illness? They got misrouted. It's not their fault.

Again, the only appropriate response is compassion and forgiveness. Also, try to help rather than blame those who stumble.

Attention: At all times, keep in mind that maybe you're wrong this time. Maybe you're the one erring.

Practice 43

Pity Rather than Blame the Wrongdoer

"As we pity the blind and the lame, so should we pity those who are blinded and lamed in their most sovereign faculties. The man who remembers this, I say, will be angry with no one, indignant with no one, revile none, blame none, hate none, offend none."

– EPICTETUS

The people who do wrong? Pity rather than blame them.

They don't do it on purpose. They are blinded and lamed in their most sovereign faculty: their mind, and thus in their ability to think straight and use reason.

These poor people! Even if what they do hurts you, know that they're blinded and don't see what they're doing. If you're able to recognize this injury, you'll be angry with none, revile none, blame none, and offend none.

That's what the Stoics ask of us: To be our best even if we get slapped in the face. And knowing that the wrongdoer is lamed in his most important faculty is an immense help.

You wouldn't judge an injured teammate when he's unable to catch a ball. In the exact same way the injured player shouldn't judge the person who tells him off. Because the offender is injured too, just not in his body but in his mind. Even if we can't see it from the outside.

The person is penalized enough for being blinded in his most important ability.

However, if you find it difficult to recognize this injury in people who hurt you, simply know this: "The person who does wrong, does wrong to themselves. The unjust person is unjust to themselves—making themselves evil."

Marcus Aurelius is making the point that ultimately people hurt themselves when they go wrong. Maybe they will feel guilt or shame after acting unjustly, and maybe they won't feel anything. It doesn't matter.

But you know by now that virtue is the highest good. If you do what's right, you'll live a happy life. And the same is true for the people who act wrong. They won't lead happy lives.

What goes around comes around.

Whenever someone wrongs you, you have several options. Maybe you judge what happened as bad and get hurt by it. Maybe you judge the wrongdoer as evil and get angry at him. Maybe you see the situation as neutral and make the best of it. And maybe you recognize that the wrongdoer is blinded in his ability to use reason, and you choose to pity rather than blame him.

It's in your power to be kind to people. It's in your power to stay true to your path and respond to evildoers with compassion, forgiveness, and kindness.

Because even if what they say or do hurts you, you know they're lamed in their most important faculty and will ultimately hurt themselves.

Practice 44

Kindness Is Strength

"Wherever there is a human being,
there is an opportunity for kindness."
– SENECA

Whenever you meet another being, it's a chance for kindness. It doesn't need to be a *human* being, it can also be cats, dogs, and other animals, even plants.

If you want to be your best, kindness is a great value to develop. And nothing can hinder you from being kind. It's always possible—smile at your neighbor in the morning, say hi to the bus driver, and thank the cashier at the supermarket.

"Kindness is invincible," says Marcus, as long as it's sincere. "For what can even the most malicious person do if you keep showing kindness?"

The next time you get treated meanly, don't fight back but accept it. Don't resist what happens. Accept it as it is and respond with tolerance and kindness, it's the best you can do. "Most rudeness, meanness, and cruelty are a mask for deep-seated weakness," says Ryan Holiday. "Kindness in these situations is only possible for people of great strength."

Be kind and show that strength.

You were born kind, says Marcus. It's your nature to act in a kind and supportive way. Remember, we're all brothers and sisters, and even if others err, we're meant to respond kindly. That's brotherly love.

What's stopping you? Ask yourself, in which situations do you want to show more kindness today? When and where do you want to gift your smile, be tolerant to erring people, share a kind and sincere *thank you*, and lend a helping hand?

Remember Seneca's words: "Wherever there is a human being, there is an opportunity for kindness." And hear him out again: "Hecato says, 'I can teach you a love potion made without any drugs, herbs, or special spell—if you would be loved, love.'"

Practice 45

How to Deal with Insults

"How much better to heal than seek revenge from injury.
Vengeance wastes a lot of time and exposes you to many
more injuries than the first that sparked it. Anger always
outlasts hurt. Best to take the opposite course. Would anyone
think it normal to return a kick to a mule or a bite to a dog?"

– SENECA

Simple yet mean remarks can ruin a whole day. But only if
we let them.

It's easy to get angry and counter with an insult. Or if we
don't agree what another person does, we might think,
"Arrgh, I'll get him for that!"

This is the worst possible response to bad behavior.

So, what's the Stoic response to insults? William Irvine
shares some strategies in a chapter on insults in his book *A
Guide to the Good Life*. Let's look at some from his book and
some others.

One strategy is to pause and ask whether what's been said
is true. "Why is it an insult," Seneca asks, "to be told what is
self-evident?"

Plus, let's ask who insulted us? If it's someone we respect, then we value her opinion and accept it as something we can actually improve on. If we don't respect the source, then why bother?

Seneca advises to look at an insulter as an overgrown child. Just as it would be foolish for a mother to get upset by remarks of her toddler, we'd be equally foolish to get hurt by insults of a childish person. People with such a flawed character don't deserve our anger, says Marcus, they only deserve our pity.

Let's remember that rational and wise people don't insult others, at least not on purpose. So if a person insults us, we can be certain this person has a flawed and immature character. Irvine compares being insulted by another person is like taking the barking of a dog personally. We'd be fools to become upset by that dog and think for the rest of the day, "Oh dear! That dog doesn't like me!"

Marcus Aurelius saw insulting people as a lesson: who not to be. "The best revenge is to be unlike him who performed the injury." The best revenge is to let it go and be a better example.

And how should we respond when confronted?

The Stoics say with humor rather than a counter insult. Make a joke, laugh it off.

It can be hard to find the right words, right? So the better strategy might be not to respond at all. Instead of reacting to an insult, says Musonius Rufus, "calmly and quietly bear what happened."

Remember the art of acquiescence: we want to accept everything as it happens. Because it's not under our control and we can't change it once it happened. Reality is as it is.

So let's not show any resistance to the insult. Don't go into reaction mode with an attack, defense, or withdrawal, but let it pass right through you. As if you were not there. Offer no resistance.

There's nobody to get hurt. In this way, you become invulnerable. The insult goes right through you. That person has no power to control how you feel.

You can, however, let that person know that their behavior is unacceptable, if you choose to. In specific situations, this might be needed. We need to teach children how to behave properly in this world. When a child or even a student disrupts the lecture by insulting the teacher or other students, then the teacher needs to reprimand the insulter to ensure the right lecture environment.

The reprimand is not an emotional reaction to the insult, but a rationally chosen action to help the insulter improve their behavior, and to ensure the right environment.

One more strategy is to keep in mind what Epictetus says: "What is insulting is not the person who abuses you or hits you, but the judgment about them that they are insulting."

We can only be insulted if we let it happen. If we don't care what others say, then we won't feel insulted. After all, other people's actions are not under our control, so they're ultimately indifferent. So let's not care too much about what others say to and about us. Why would they know? Hear out Marcus on this: "I'm constantly amazed by how easily we love ourselves above all others, yet we put more stock in the opinions of others than in our own estimation of self . . . How much credence we give to the opinions our peers have of us and how little to our very own!"

Take that to heart and don't take other people's opinions about you too seriously. Train yourself to endure their insults.

You'll get more effective at reacting in appropriate ways, you'll get stronger, and you might even become invincible, says Epictetus: "Who then is invincible? The one who cannot be upset by anything outside their reasoned choice."

Practice 46

Scratches Happen In Training

"When your sparring partner scratches or head-butts you, you
don't then make a show of it, or protest, or view him with
suspicion or as plotting against you. And yet you keep an eye
on him, not as an enemy or with suspicion, but with a healthy
avoidance. You should act this way with all things in life.
We should give a pass to many things with our fellow
trainees. For, as I've said, it's possible
to avoid without suspicion or hate."

– MARCUS AURELIUS

See each day and every situation as a training exercise. You
will accept things quicker even if they're annoying—it's just
training.

Scratches happen. Don't blame your sparring partner.
Don't blame the event. We're all just training. Things go
wrong. People act like jerks.

The stakes suddenly become much lower. We interpret
mistakes more generously. We stretch a point an extra time.
We're way more resilient that way.

Imagine the opposite. Seeing every situation as the championship was on the line . . . You'd be on tenterhooks all the time, and react to every tiny thing. It's much smarter to be easy and shake off minor blows with a simple nod. Just dust it off as training. Nothing happened. Move on.

You don't want to be the person who gets enraged over scratches. They take things so seriously it seems ridiculous from the outside. They think that barely visible spot ruins their looks, that dirty remark is worth a fight, or that leftover sip of milk is a reason to lose their mind.

Look, these things might be important to you, but that's no reason to blow a gasket. Remain calm, scratches happen. Smile and move on. And if appropriate, inform others about your opinion on how to eat ice cream, talk to people, and how much milk is fine to leave in the bottle.

"The art of living is more like wrestling than dancing," as encountered in Chapter 1, "because an artful life requires being prepared to meet and withstand sudden and unexpected attacks."

Marcus reminds us to be prepared for sudden slaps. All these hits and blows life throws at us are opportunities for practice. Each slap contains the chance to stay calm and strengthen who you want to be, but also the risk to go ballistic and become more of who you don't want to be.

You're a warrior. Nothing and nobody can throw you off balance easily. You're ready to deal with some punches and side-kicks. Such is life. Even better, knowing that these kicks make you stronger, you rub your hands together and look forward to them. They cannot come unexpected and hard enough.

You want to be strong. You want to handle yourself in the face of adversity. You want to be unshakable in the midst of a storm. You want to remain cool when others panic.

So you simply can't afford to turn your head to every scratch. It's just training. Smile and move on.

Practice 47

Don't Abandon Others nor Yourself

"As you move forward along the path of reason, people will stand in your way. They will never be able to keep you from doing what's sound, so don't let them knock out your goodwill for them. Keep a steady watch on both fronts, not only for well-based judgments and actions, but also for gentleness with those who would obstruct our path or create other difficulties. For getting angry is also a weakness, just as much as abandoning the task or surrendering under panic. For doing either is an equal desertion—the one by shrinking back and the other by estrangement from family and friend."

– MARCUS AURELIUS

You're a reader. As a reader, you learn new ideas and different ways to approach and do things. You put into practice what resonates with you the most and as a consequence you ditch your old behavior and install the newly learned.

The point is, you change over time. You don't stick to old habits just because it's convenient, you want to grow and try new ways, and keep those that work.

A few years back, I learned a lot about milk and dairy foods and decided to ditch it for the good. This change affected mainly me. On a few occasions, it could have affected others as well, for example when I would have told my dad, "Sorry, I can't eat this omelet because you put some milk in it." Or when I would have said strictly no to every desert or food with a finger cup of milk in it.

I chose not to go down that path for simplicity reasons. For myself and others. I didn't want to explain myself every time when I didn't eat a certain food with a tiny amount of milk in it. Plus, some people would have felt like making something especially for me, and I didn't want that. Also, I drank a lot of milk for all my life and it was never an issue, so why make a drama for just a sip?

So, with milk, this was a smooth change because it mainly affected myself and I chose not to go 100% strict.

But with other changes, we might encounter stronger headwinds. "As you move forward along the path of reason," Marcus says, "people will stand in your way." When you're installing new habits and try to make progress, others might not be as quick or even willing to follow along.

Now it's our challenge not to abandon our new path and, at the same time, not to abandon our friends and family.

Ryan Holiday compares it to a diet: When everyone in your clique is eating unhealthy, then there's a natural alignment. But if, after reading some book, you choose to start eating healthy, suddenly there are opposing agendas. Now there's an argument about where to eat.

"Just as you must not abandon your new path simply because other people may have a problem with it," Ryan says, "you must not abandon those other folks either. Don't simply write them off or leave them in the dust. Don't get mad or fight with them. After all, they're at the same place you were not long ago."

Just because you read *Wheat Belly* and from one day to another choose not to eat gluten anymore, you cannot abandon all your friends for still eating gluten. I mean, just a few days ago it was you who organized pizza night.

So, we shouldn't abandon others just because we chose to change, but we also shouldn't abandon our new path. That's a challenge we'll all face sooner or later, not necessarily with the gluten, but maybe with other ideas and values.

Eating less (or no) meat, wasting less time playing video games, watching less news, spending more time outdoors, reading more, buying less material stuff, working out more often, stopping binge-drinking every weekend, or complaining less.

Now it's a tough challenge to stick to your new path and not to abandon others. Because the differences might be huge. But, if you try and give it some time, I'm sure you'll figure a way out. Choose to bring your own food to pizza night, prepare to fast if necessary, teach others about your reasons, and maybe compromise once a month.

Remain kind and patient with others, after all, you were at the same place not long ago.

Find ways to stick to your new path. Don't bend your values.

Practice 48

For Such a Small Price, Buy Tranquility

"Starting with things of little value—a bit of spilled oil, a little stolen wine—repeat to yourself: 'For such a small price I buy tranquility and peace of mind.'"

– EPICTETUS

This is one of my favorite Stoic ideas.

"I buy tranquility instead." This sentence saved me countless times from getting angry and irritated. How often do we get angry at trifles? How often do we lose our mind for something as insignificant as a fart in the bathroom?

We let small things arouse our anger, and our consequential actions arouse anger in others, and so forth. The Stoics want to stay calm even in the midst of a storm, and yet we go crazy when our roomie forgets to do the dishes, leaves skid marks behind in the toilet, or doesn't do his chores.

It obviously doesn't need to be this way. Before you react to whatever arouses anger within, say to yourself: "I buy tranquility instead." Then smile, do what needs to get done, and move on with your life.

Nothing happened. You will soon realize that the small things that usually irritate you are not worth the hassle. Just swallow whatever feelings arise within and move on. This will save you a ton of nerves and energy.

The main challenge is this: We need to be aware of the arising feelings in the first place. So we need to be able to step in between stimulus and automatic response. And once we're in that gap, we need to have the self-discipline to actually buy tranquility and not react at all.

The more often you're able to buy tranquility, the easier it'll get. And you'll become able to even buy tranquility in more challenging situations.

Skid marks are easy, it just takes a few seconds to clean up. Red wine on your white dress is still easy, it's just a dress. A late and decisive equalizer against your favorite team is still manageable, it's just a game. A cheating boyfriend is much more challenging, because it'll take some grieve and anger work.

The point is, the more you practice buying tranquility, the better you'll get. Up to the moment you'll be able to buy tranquility in the midst of a hellfire.

Ultimately, this all comes down to the Stoic principle that it's not events that upset us, but our judgment about those events. If we recognize our power, and bring enough awareness and discipline into challenging situations, then we're on our way to become an emotionally resilient and steadfast person.

If that's the path you want to go, ask yourself: "In which situations could I buy tranquility more often?"

Practice 49

Put Yourself in Other People's Shoes

"When you face someone's insults, hatred, whatever . . . look at his soul. Get inside him. Look at what sort of person he is. You'll find you don't need to strain to impress him."
– MARCUS AURELIUS

We're often quick to judge.

- The father on the train who doesn't tell his loud kids to be quiet—we say he doesn't have the faintest idea of being a father.
- The driver who runs all the red lights—we're quick to judge him as a jerk.
- The mother who tells us off at the playground—we think she's completely mad.

Now, in most cases, we don't know much about the other person, and yet we judge them, and complain about them.

The Stoics advise us to put ourselves in the other person's shoes, to take their perspective before passing a judgment.

We should enter their minds, says Marcus. And see what they're like. What they're working at. And what evokes their love and admiration. "Imagine their souls stripped bare." We should really try to put ourselves in their perspective before we judge them.

For the Stoics, it's more important to love than to be loved. They train themselves to deal with challenging people, particularly to avoid responding impulsively and with anger.

That's why we should try to step into their shoes and try to understand their reason behind their action. And maybe we'll see their reason. Maybe we'll understand them. And maybe we'll conclude they're mistaken about their reason.

Remember the father with the loud kids on the train? The one we said doesn't have the faintest idea of being a father? Good. Let me tell you a quick story about this man and his kids, slightly adapted from the original story Stephen Covey tells in his *The 7 Habits of Highly Effective People*.

So this father is sitting on the train, his face hidden behind both hands, looking like a picture of misery. His two kids are running around and screaming loudly. People get annoyed by them. You, too, are getting annoyed and think the father should look after his kids better. You get up and approach the man:

"Excuse me, sir, your kids are very loud. Could you please tell them to be quiet?"

"Oh sorry," he responds. "I just don't know what to do. We've just come from the hospital where their mom died."

Whoops!

What a shift in perspective, right?

We judge people but don't know the situation they're in. We don't know their backstory, we don't know why they do what they do. We basically know nothing about them.

Let's take the Stoics' advice by heart and always take a second before we judge others. Put yourself in their shoes, and think about possible reasons why they act the way they do. Maybe you'd do the same if you were in their situation. Who knows?

Practice 50

Choose Your Company Well

"Avoid fraternizing with non-philosophers. If you must,
though, be careful not to sink to their level; because, you
know, if a companion is dirty, his friends cannot help but get
a little dirty too, no matter how clean they started out."

– EPICTETUS

We can't always choose the people we're dealing with.
That's why the Stoics offer so many strategies to deal with
challenging people.

But to a certain degree, we can choose our company. We
can choose who we want to spend most of our leisure time
with. We can choose which events we attend, and who to go
with.

As Epictetus says, if our companions are dirty, we might
get dirty as well. This is why Seneca warns us that vices are
contagious—they spread like wildfire but don't get noticed.

That's peer pressure 101—we do things we usually
wouldn't do. We suddenly behave contrary to our values. We
adapt to the people we surround ourselves with. Maybe

you've heard Jim Rohn's famous idea before: "You are the average of the five people you spend most time with."

That's why we should choose our friends carefully. They have the power to pull you either down or up to their level. You either get better, thanks to the people you spend time with, or you get worse because of them.

"Avoid feasting with low people. Those who are not modest even when sober become much more recklessly impudent after drinking." Seneca makes a fair point. His solution?

"Associate with people who are likely to improve you."

Now, you might have people you love, but who also drag you down with their attitudes, even when sober. They're lazy. They don't care much about moral standards. They aren't interested in improving themselves, not to mention Stoicism. They think that's the most boring and annoying idea you've ever shared with them.

What to do with those people? Epictetus says, "The key is to keep company only with people who uplift you, whose presence calls forth your best."

So, either they're willing to change for the better, or you simply spend less time with them. If your friends don't make you better, don't encourage you to push forward, don't even support you in your ambitious pursuit of moral improvement, then it's time to ditch them.

You don't need to break up and never see them again, but you can consciously spend less time with them. And you can always talk to people, some will be all ears to hear about your newly gained knowledge, ideas, and activities.

Seneca also advises to spend less time with people who always complain: The companion "who is always upset and bemoans everything is a foe to tranquility."

Apart from spending *less* time with the complaining and those who drag us down, we should try to spend *more* time with people who are likely to make us better. This makes total sense, if you spend time with an exemplar, you're more likely to become like this person.

Where do you find people who'll improve you? Be creative. Try a yoga class, attend TED talks or other lectures, join a book club or language course or whatever. I'm sure there are many people out there you can learn from.

Remember, though, you can be annoying too. We all have failings. So while thinking about surrounding ourselves with better people, we must not forget that we're flawed, too. We make mistakes, we're not always fair, and we can be nagging. Keep that in mind.

In conclusion, the idea to choose your company well is not only about the people you spend the lion's share of your time with, but also about not wasting your precious time. Temptation and timewasters are lurking around the corner, so we need to pay attention to what we're doing and who we're doing it with.

Generally, if you want to be the best you can be, surround yourself with the best people. If you want to avoid getting angry and annoyed, don't spend time with people who are likely to make you angry and annoyed.

Practice 51

Don't Judge But Yourself

"Someone bathes in haste; don't say he bathes badly, but in haste. Someone drinks a lot of wine; don't say he drinks badly, but a lot. Until you know their reasons, how do you know that their actions are vicious? This will save you from perceiving one thing clearly, but then assenting to something different."

– EPICTETUS

Our minds are very quick to judge.

We label people on the basis of very little information. We're prejudiced. Oh, he's a teacher. Oh, she's a woman. Oh, look at those shoes he's wearing.

We find mistakes in others a dime a dozen.

Look, most of the times we don't *want* to judge others so rapidly, it just happens automatically, these judgments pop up magically in our minds.

However, we must take responsibility for our judgments. Because we can choose to go with them or not. So even if the mind tells you this man is a bad father for not watching his kids, you can choose to accept this notion or not.

You have the power to pause and look at the situation objectively. What do you know about this man? What's the situation exactly?

Refuse to accept all that's other than objective. Stick to the facts and describe the situation in a neutral way. Without adding any value to it.

Remember, you are only free if you can look at external events with indifference. And immediately adding value to an event is all but indifferent.

We must distinguish between the facts and our added value judgments. What's the fact? What did I add?

The key to be able to do that is to postpone our reaction. "Wait for me a little, impression . . . let me put you to the test."

And now instead of actually testing the impression—which usually isn't important anyway—you remind yourself of your goal in life. If you're taking any of the philosophy's advice to heart, then your goal is to improve yourself, to get better, to express your highest version of yourself.

"Let philosophy scrape off your own faults, rather than be a way to rail against the faults of others."

Seneca reminds us here of what philosophy is for: we want to scrape off our own faults. The focus is inward. To make yourself better and to leave other people to that task for themselves. Everybody must go their own way.

Your faults are in your control. Other people's faults are not. You scrape off your faults, and let other people scrape off theirs for themselves.

We must not forget why we engage in philosophy in the first place: to improve ourselves. It's not a tool to correct others. This will only cause pain and suffering.

Leave other people to their faults. Nothing in Stoicism empowers us to judge them—only to accept and love them as they are. Let's focus inward. There's enough to correct in ourselves.

Now pause for a moment and imagine the world if we all abstained from hasty judgments and rather focused on scraping off our own faults. What do you see?

Practice 52

Do Good, Not Only No Evil

"Often injustice lies in what you aren't doing,
not only in what you are doing."
– MARCUS AURELIUS

Sure, it's great if you don't bully co-workers. But if you just stand there and watch, and maybe even laugh at the bully's mean remarks, then you're not any better than the bully.

Stop the immature behavior. Step in between, help the bullied. A little courage, and do what's right.

It's when good citizens decline to get involved when evil will triumph. There's a famous saying: "The only thing necessary for the triumph of evil is for good men to do nothing."

Don't be the person who does nothing. There's nothing you can lose. If you lead as an example, many more will follow. People just need a leader. You can be that leader.

I bet you've witnessed this scene: One rude person annoys everyone else.

It's classic. Everybody is looking at this pain in the neck, and they start getting angry inside, but no one will stop the madness. Until a hero enters the scene, walks up to the madman, tells him something, and voilà, problem solved.

Everybody could have done it. But nobody thought he's the right one to do it. Or none had the courage to confront the nag.

But there's not always a hero, and the madness goes on until the game is over, the movie is finished, or you go home after a nerve-wracking evening.

Look, I know it's not easy to head for and confront annoying people, especially if it could be dangerous for you—nobody asks you to fight a knifeman.

Start with small things. The loud chewer sitting next to you on the train. Your co-worker with the terrible breath. Or the guy in the sauna who can't close the door.

It took me two long minutes and some nerves to tell that guy to please close the sauna door. Instead of asking him immediately to close the door behind him, I fought with myself for two minutes, got a bit angry at him, and realized how ridiculous my thoughts and behavior were.

Next time, I'll be quicker to ask for what I think are common manners. Please queue up like everybody else. Please turn down the volume. Please close the door.

Agreed, this may sound a bit like being a control-freak. But isn't it much smarter to confront, risk an awkward situation, but maybe even help this person rather than getting pissed off and raging inside and yet doing nothing?

It's funny how we choose to be angry at strangers rather than politely asking them to stop or change. Ryan Holiday says it well: "We don't just want people to be better, we expect it to magically happen—that we can simply will other people to change, burning holes into their skull with our angry stare."

Marcus Aurelius reminds himself and us to use reason in such situations: "Are you angry when someone's armpits stink or when their breath is bad? What would be the point? Having such a mouth and such armpits, there's going to be a smell emanating. You say, they must have sense, can't they tell how they are offending others? Well, you have sense, too, congratulations! So, use your natural reason to awaken theirs, show them, call it out. If the person will listen, you will have cured them without useless anger. No drama nor unseemly show required."

For me it's the same. It's easier to say nothing and be bitter about it than to be brave, confront it, and then maybe be happy about it.

As aspiring Stoics, however, we should rather muster all our courage and try to help the situation for all participants. If you had a bad breath, wouldn't you like to be informed about it? If you smell, wouldn't you like to know?

The annoying person might be unaware of it. So why not point it out and give them the chance to change? And at the same time giving you the chance for peace of mind?

It's not enough to just not do evil. We must be a force for the good in the world, even in minor situations. As well as we can.

Practice 53

Say Only What's Not Better Left Unsaid

"Let silence be your goal for the most part; say only what is necessary, and be brief about it. On the rare occasions when you're called upon to speak, then speak, but never about banalities like gladiators, horses, sports, food and drink—common-place stuff. Above all don't gossip about people, praising, blaming or comparing them."

– EPICTETUS

Next time you're speaking with others, observe the conversation. You'll see that everybody talks about themselves. Whatever the topic, everybody will find something from their own life to add to the conversation.

That's what we do. We like to talk about ourselves. So we don't really listen to what's being said, but we prepare for when it's our turn.

And if we speak about others, then it's most certainly about something they don't do well. We gossip. We compare ourselves to others in what we think we're better. If we think about it, indulging in gossip and judging people who aren't present to defend themselves doesn't seem to be a fair thing to do.

The Stoics are clear on this: Don't gossip. Don't blame. Don't complain. Don't talk too much. Especially not about what's not meaningful.

"In your conversation, don't dwell at excessive length on your own deeds or adventures." Epictetus is strict: don't tell excessive stories. "Just because you enjoy recounting your exploits doesn't mean that others derive the same pleasure from hearing about them."

Nobody wants to hear your exaggerated high school, sports, and party stories. It's annoying and self-absorbed. You might feel great because you're at the center of the conversation—but how is it for everyone else? Sure, they smile and don't say much, but how do they really feel?

Marcus Aurelius advises to speak only what you think is just, and always do so with kindness, modesty, and sincerity.

The point is: Speak only when you're certain that what you'll say isn't better left unsaid.

Also, put into practice what you preach. Speak with your actions more than with your words.

This idea is very simple to put into practice. Go into a conversation with the intention to listen for the most part. Observe what they talk about. Observe within yourself the urge to say something (probably it'll be self-related), and then only say it when it's not better left unsaid.

Connect with people. Don't perform for them. Let them do most of the talking. Enjoy listening.

Practice 54

Listen with the Intent to Understand

"Acquire the habit of attending carefully to what is being said
by another, and of entering, so far as possible,
into the mind of the speaker."

– MARCUS AURELIUS

The Stoics advise to listen rather than speak.

And if you listen, you should pay attention to what's being said so you understand what the speaker is trying to express. That way, you acknowledge the other person's values and autonomy.

The goal when you enter a conversation is to understand what the other person wants to tell you. You listen with the intent to understand. That's called *empathic listening*. And it'll massively improve your relationships.

Resist the urge to speak. Accept that something within you always wants to respond immediately. It wants to add something to the conversation. But often, that's not necessary and even detrimental to the conversation. Marcus describes it well: "In conversation, one should attend closely to what is being said, and with regard to every impulse attend to what arises from it; in the latter case, to see from the first what end it has in view, and in the former, to keep careful watch on what people are meaning to say."

Your main question is: What does the other person try to express?

Listen to what's being said and take accompanying emotions into consideration as well. That's how you foster understanding and connection between you and the speaker.

Remember the founder of Stoicism? Zeno of Citium, the shipwreck guy? The Greek biographer Diogenes Laertius wrote that Zeno said to some youngster talking nonsense: "The reason why we have two ears and only one mouth is so we might listen more and talk less."

In conversation, make it a rule to hold your fire. Be the person who listens most of the time, and says only what improves the conversation. People will benefit even if they don't say so. And you not only improve your empathic listening skills, but more generally your conversation and observation skills, and on top of that your relationships.

As Zeno famously said, "Better to trip with the feet than with the tongue."

Practice 55

Lead by Example

"Waste no more time arguing about what a
good man should be. Be one."
– MARCUS AURELIUS

Lead with your actions. Be the example. An active role model easily beats a lecture.

Don't instruct, but silently demonstrate. Start with the face in the mirror. "Act on your principles," says Epictetus, "For instance, at a banquet do not say how one ought to eat, but eat as you ought."

There's great danger, he says, to talk about what you've learned. Because you might vomit up what's not yet digested. "For even sheep do not vomit up their grass and show to the shepherds how much they have eaten; but when they have internally digested the pasture, they produce externally wool and milk."

In the same way, we shouldn't talk about what isn't yet fully digested, but show the acts which come from digesting the theory. Show, don't tell, what you've learned.

So that when someone treats you rudely, you can show what you've learned and respond with kindness and forgiveness. For if you respond with rudeness, it only proves you haven't learned anything yet. You're the same as the other.

But if you manage to remain calm and considered, and choose a tolerant and compassionate response, then you're setting an example. And others will follow. Maybe even the evildoer.

The Stoics say we must set standards, and then live by them. It's the work of philosophy to examine and uphold the standards, "but the work of a truly good person is in using those standards when they know them."

Epictetus couldn't be clearer—we must live by the standards we know.

Have you admired any of the ideas presented in this book? Have you agreed with some of them? Then be the truly good person who also lives by what she or he knows.

Ask yourself: "Who do I want to be in the world out there?"

And then live by it. If you want to be kind, then be kind. If you want to be patient, then be patient. If you want to be honest, then be honest.

If you live by your beliefs and standards you'll be in a harmony called *cognitive consonance*. You think a way and act that way too. That feels great.

Put into practice what you believe is right.

Lead by example and others will follow. People follow action more than instruction. So actively demonstrate what you think is the best thing to do. As they say: Be the change you want to see in the world.

"Waste no more time arguing about what a good man should be. Be one."

Acknowledgments

First of all, I'd like to thank you, the reader, for giving an unknown first-time author the chance to prove himself. *Thank* you for your time. I sincerely appreciate it.

Nils, my brother, business partner, and friend, *merci* for your endless support. Without you, this book would have never seen the light of day.

Anastasia, our Greek artist, *efharisto* for your stunning drawings. They add just the right taste.

Ryan Holiday, you don't know me, but I'm one of many you introduced to this wonderful philosophy. *Thanks* for your inspiration and hard work.

And thanks to all the people who supported me on this arduous journey. The struggle was well worth it.

Thank You!

Selected Bibliography

Covey, Stephen R. *The 7 Habits of Highly Effective People: Powerful Lessons in Personal Change*. London: Pocket Books, 2004.

Diogenes Laertius. *Lives of the Eminent Philosophers*. Vol. 2. Translated by R.D. Hicks. Cambridge, MA: Harvard University Press, 1925.

Epictetus. *Discourses*. http://classics.mit.edu/Epictetus/discourses.html.

Epictetus. *Enchiridion*. Translated by George Long. New York: Dover Publications, 2004.

Evans, Jules. *Seneca and the Art of Managing Expectations*. https://www.cbu.ca/wp-content/uploads/2017/01/8-Why-is-it-important-to-Manage-our-Expectations.pdf.

Frankl, Viktor. *Man's Search for Meaning*. Boston, MA: Beacon Press, 2006.

Hadot, Pierre. *Philosophy as a Way of Life*. Edited by Arnold I. Davidson. Cambridge, MA: Blackwell, 1995.

Hadot, Pierre. *The Inner Citadel: The Meditations of Marcus Aurelius*. Cambridge, MA: Harvard University Press, 1998.

Holiday, Ryan. *The Obstacle Is the Way: The Art of Turning Adversity to Advantage*. London: Profile Books, 2015.

Holiday, Ryan., and Stephen Hanselmann. *The Daily Stoic: 366 Meditations on Wisdom, Perseverance, and the Art of Living*. New York: Portfolio, 2016.

Irvine, William B. *A Guide to the Good Life*. New York: Oxford University Press, 2008.

Johnson, Brian. https://www.optimize.me/plus-one/how-to-high-five-your-inner-daimon/.

Katie, Byron, and Stephen Mitchell. *Loving What Is: Four Questions that Can Change Your Life. New York:* Harmony Books, 2002.

Long, A. A. *Epictetus: A Stoic and Socratic Guide to Life.* Oxford: Clarendon Press, 2002.

Marcus Aurelius. *Meditations.* London: Penguin Group, 2006.

Millman, Dan. *Way of the Peaceful Warrior: A Book that Changes Lives.* Novato, CA: New World Library, 2000.

Musonius Rufus. *The Lectures and Sayings of Musonius Rufus.* Translated by Cynthia King. Createspace, 2011.

Pigliucci, Massimo. *How to Be a Stoic: Ancient Wisdom for Modern Living.* London: Rider, 2017.

Robertson, Donald. *Stoicism and the Art of Happiness: Ancient Tips for Modern Challenges.* London: Hodder & Stoughton, 2013.

Robertson, Donald. *The Philosophy of Cognitive Behavioural Therapy (CBT).* London: Karnac, 2010.

Seneca. *Dialogues and Letters.* Edited and translated by C.D.N. Costa. London: Penguin Group, 2005.

Seneca. *Letters from a Stoic.* London: Penguin Group, 2004.

Seneca. *Moral Essays.* Vol. 1. Translated by John W. Basore. Cambridge, MA: Harvard University Press, 1928.

Stephens, William O. "Stoic Ethics." *Internet Encyclopedia of Philosophy,* http://www.iep.utm.edu/stoiceth/.

Taleb, Nassim N. *Antifragile: Things that Gain from Disorder.* New York: Random House, 2012.

Want More?

My brother Nils and I are voracious readers and try to get better every day. Stoicism helps, Positive Psychology helps, overcoming procrastination helps, and yet, we're still struggling. That's ok. Just get up, rub off the dust, look ahead and keep moving.

We write for a small army of remarkable people at NJlifehacks.com and share what we find most useful in our distracting world.

If you'd like to join us and get fresh articles delivered to your inbox every week, sign up at NJlifehacks.com.

Or you can just send me an e-mail at jonas@njlifehacks.com and tell me you want to get inside (just put Fresh Articles in the subject line).